FROM DUST & RABBITS

The First Eighty Years

Len Glare

ECHO BOOKS

First published in 2017 by Barrallier Books Pty Ltd,
trading as Echo Books

Registered Office: 35-37 Gordon Avenue, West Geelong,
Victoria 3220, Australia.

www.echobooks.com.au

Copyright ©Len Glare

National Library of Australia Cataloguing-in-Publication entry.

Creator: Glare, Len, author.

Title: From dust and rabbits : the first eighty years / Len Glare.

ISBN: 9780995436480 (paperback)

Subjects: Glare, Len. Glare, Len--Family. Australia--Officials and employees--Biography. Public service employment--Australia. Domestic relations courts--Australia. Domestic relations courts--Australia.Book layout and design by Peter Gamble, Canberra.

Set in Garamond Premier Pro Display, 12/17.

www.echobooks.com.au

Front cover image: *Dust Storm 1937.* Source Mallee Lands Latrobe University

For my late parents, George and Freda Glare, who gave me a strong base and sound values and for my wonderful family for their love and support.

Thanks to Professor Brij Vilash Lal AM for his invaluable advice and for taking such an interest in my project.

Foreword

The Hon. Alastair Nicholson AO RFD QC
(Former Chief Justice of the Family Court of Australia
and Former Judge Advocate-General of the Australian Defence Force)

I have had the honour of knowing Len Glare and his late wife Barbara since the 1980's but our close association did not begin until he accepted the position of Chief Executive Officer of the Family Court of Australia in late 1989, with effect from 1 January 1990.

The title of his book, *From Dust and Rabbits* is particularly apt as anyone who is familiar with Hopetoun and the Mallee country of western Victoria can attest. Dust storms were frequent and rabbit was a principal item of diet. Some of my own forebears came from near this area, which has always provided a struggle to those who live there. It had been a particular struggle for those like Len's parents, who had lived through the Great Depression of the 1930's and the war years.

To get by in the Mallee required strength, determination and a high degree of self-discipline as life was a constant battle as the story of Len, his parents and siblings attests. Even so there would not be too many Mallee families of that era that could have brought up two sons, one of whom attained high levels in the Federal Public Service as Len did and another Kel, who worked his way through the ranks of Victoria Police to become Chief Commissioner of Police. The third son, Rob, became Victorian Secretary of the Australian Education Union. It says a lot for the parents and the boys themselves.

Len's is a classic Australian story of a young man from a poor but supportive family, who overcame all sorts of obstacles to have an extraordinary career. That career took him to the highest levels of the Public Service and to head the administration of the then largest superior court in Australia, the Family Court.

The book records that he left school at 14 to join the Post Office and become a junior postal officer in Hopetoun and in this way his public service career commenced in 1949. He did so at the urging of his parents, who were anxious for their sons to obtain the security that a public service job then offered. At age 16 he went to Melbourne for further training and became a qualified telegraphist and Morse code operator. He gives a fascinating and entertaining account of life as a telegraphist in those days and also of living alone as a young man in Melbourne. Following a spell in RAAF National Service he returned to the Post Office and met his wife Barbara and they married in 1956.

The book goes on to describe in classic fashion his long climb in the Public Service which must have involved extremely hard work to obtain the necessary qualifications while at the same time having responsibility for a young and growing family. It also provides a great insight into the workings of the Public Service and the opportunities that it could then provide to people with the skills and determination to take advantage of them as Len did.

Very unusually for a person of his training and background, he and the family moved to Canberra where he joined the Attorney-General's Department and eventually became Deputy Secretary.

Some of the more entertaining matters discussed are his relationship with various political figures, including ten Attorneys-General. A highlight was his involvement at the direction of Gareth Evans in organising spy flights by the RAAF over Tasmania during the dams dispute. Others relate to Lionel Murphy, Kep Enderby, Peter Durack and more.

Another interesting area covers his involvement in the investigation of the attacks on judges of the Family Court in the early 1980's which is of topical interest given the fact that charges have been laid recently in relation to these offences.

Because I only knew him in a later period of his extraordinary career, it was not until I read this book that I came to appreciate the factors that made him the person that I came to know and the highly competent CEO that he proved to be.

When I came to the Family Court in 1988, it became obvious to me that it was an administrative nightmare, not through any fault of the Principal Registrar and Registrars of the Court, who then administered it under the direction of the Attorney-General's Department, but because the structure was wrong and the division of administrative responsibilities with the Department unworkable.

In fairness, it must be said that many courts were badly administered in those days and the profession of court administration that we now have was then in its infancy. The situation was further complicated by the very limited powers of the Chief Justice to have any involvement in court administration other than in respect of the judiciary and the fact that administrative power lay with the Department.

At the time of Len's appointment, amendments to the relevant legislation came into effect which enabled the Court to administer its own affairs and have its own budget and which provided for the appointment of a CEO. This provided a remarkable opportunity to renovate its administration, subject to obtaining the services of a competent CEO to take advantage of that opportunity.

The second stroke of good fortune was that the Court obtained Len's services as CEO, because he was one of the few people within the Attorney-General's Department who was not only competent but experienced in administration generally and with a sound knowledge of courts administration as well. Not only was he competent, but I think it fair to say that he pioneered the emerging profession of court administration in Australia.

Len was a classic public servant in the best sense of that description. He was intelligent, independent and loyal. He did not hesitate to criticise decisions and suggest alternatives, but when taken he would implement them without further complaint.

It was not such good fortune for Len to come to the Court, as he describes in the book, only becoming available as the result of an extraordinary decision by the incoming Secretary of the Attorney-General's Department that it should not have non-lawyers in senior positions like that of Deputy Secretary, which Len as a non-lawyer then occupied.

The decision was extraordinary on several counts. First, the Department lacked anyone with the sort of administrative experience that Len could offer and secondly that it came at a time of a wholesale restructure of that Department and the loss of many other experienced people from which it still suffers.

Coinciding with Len's appointment to the Court an extensive review of its administration was undertaken by a team led by the Hon Neil Buckley and those recommendations were eventually put into effect, despite opposition from the Attorney-General's Department.

There followed an extensive and successful ten-year association between Len and myself and a vast improvement of the Court's administration under his direction as CEO. As he correctly recounts, we had a very close and co-operative relationship and formed a friendship which I still treasure.

The Court had always suffered from parochial attitudes within its separate registries, reflecting practices of the Supreme Court in States and Territories from whom its judges and staff were drawn. These practices were gradually abolished; skilled administrative staff were engaged to replace registrars as the court managers and the court began to face its problems on an Australia-wide basis.

Len was largely responsible for the successful implementation of these changes.

One of the great strengths of the Family Court was its counselling service and very early in Len's term and with his concurrence, we took a decision that at least half of counselling work should be undertaken before any legal proceedings were commenced. Such counselling was free and was startlingly successful with about 60% of cases resolving without litigation. This provided a great service to the parents and children who were our clients and helped remove the anguish from many cases.

That assisted with another problem that the Court faced which was that it had insufficient judges to deal with its workload and its Deputy Registrars and Registrars lacked the power to make many interim type orders, thus overloading judges with unnecessary work.

With Len's help we also devised a scheme for the appointment of Senior Registrars who could undertake the burden of this work and this proved to be immediately successful. This was undertaken with the co-operation of the Attorney-General and his Department.

However, as Len mentions in the book, I developed an unfortunate relationship with the Howard Government and its Attorney-General, Daryl Williams, for reasons that I am unable to understand.

Whatever the cause, this system was dismantled at the instance of the Government and replaced by a Court first named the Federal Magistrates Court and now the Federal Circuit Court, which as Len points out, proved to be hugely expensive and has still not properly addressed the problem of those conducting trials being overloaded with unnecessary work.

Another unfortunate Government decision was an entirely vicious cut to Family Court finances in 1997 over and above the efficiency dividend applied to other Departments and instrumentalities. This in turn led to the Court being forced to withdraw from pre-filing counselling because of reductions in counselling personnel brought about by this decision. Such counselling is now provided by non-government organisations and is no longer free of charge.

Despite these setbacks I continued to be strongly supported by Len in the provision of better services to the community by the Court

Len contributed to many other improvements in the areas of Court security, computerisation, court buildings and industrial relations and provided a steady hand to represent the Court in the myriad of Parliamentary Inquiries and Estimates Committee hearings to which the Court was subject.

The book goes on to describe Len's life after the Court, and the tragic loss of his beloved wife Barbara. His life remains a very full one and he has recently remarried and is very proud of his family and their achievements.

Overall this is a book well worth reading and describes the life of an Australian who I have been proud to call a colleague and friend.

Contents

Foreword	v
Part One—Mallee Beginnings	
Dust	1
Making Ends Meet	19
Diversions	25
Part Two—Transition from the Farm	
Town Life	35
Local Culture	43
Part Three—A Career is Launched	
Finding a Job	47
The Big Smoke	51
The Chief Telegraph Office	55
Part Four—Time Out for National Service	
National Service Training	63
Resuming Civilian Life	69
Part Five—Climbing the Career Ladder	
Traineeship	83
Central Office, Postmaster-General's Department	85
Headhunted to Canberra	93
Joining the Senior Executive Service	99

Cyclone Tracy	103
First Overseas Experience	107
Another Career Step	115
Senior Executive Fellowship	121
Part Six—Attorney's-General and other Interesting Characters	
Attorney's-General and Spy Flights Over Tasmania	131
Other interesting characters	149
Part Seven—Parliamentary Committees and Advising	
Giving Evidence	157
Advising in Parliament	165
Part Eight—Court Security	
Anticipating Trouble	169
Worst Fears	175
Part Nine—Observations on Public Service	
Lessons from Experience	181
Part Ten—Family Court of Australia	
Shaping a New Administration	187
The Nature of Family Law Jurisdiction	193
International Experience	195
Indigenous Initiatives of the Court	201
Fifty Years Service	203
East Timor	205
Media	209
Statutory Senility and Retirement	211
Part Eleven—Family	
Siblings	217
Children	221
Part Twelve—Post Retirement	
Keeping Busy	227
My Great Loss	233
Soldiering On	237
Part Thirteen—A Fortunate Life	
Reflection	251

Part One
Mallee Beginnings

Dust

It was the 18th of December 1934. The western sky began to grow menacing low down to the horizon; it became darker and more ominous. Gradually the great dust cloud came overhead but high in the sky so that it obliterated the sun long before the ground level front of the Mallee dust storm arrived. Half an hour or so later the blinding, suffocating, dust cloud arrived bringing with it high winds so that debris swirled through the air in near darkness. Visibility was just a few yards. It was a natural phenomenon that I was to see many times during my childhood but of this one I knew nothing. During this dust storm I was born, Leonard George Glare, at the Hopetoun Bush Nursing Hospital in north-western Victoria.

This was an isolated and remote part of Australia in those days being 425 kilometres from Melbourne and on the southern edge of the Mallee desert. A harsh dry climate where the landscape is flat and the soil mostly sandy as a result of once being under the sea. Great sand dunes abound. The predominant vegetation is Mallee eucalypt of many varieties. They are low growing with multiple stems coming from a large lignotuber that stores water to sustain the tree in dry times. These lignotubers, called Mallee roots, were highly prized for firewood. The area has very high temperatures in summer and some frosts in winter which is when most of the rain falls. Surface water and running streams are rare.

Mallee dust storms occurred mainly because the early farmers imported their northern hemisphere farming methods to the new country where burning the wheat stubble and frequently ploughing the soil caused instability in the topsoil so that the wind could pick it up easily and blow it over great distances. Eventually, farmers learned to turn the stubble in to hold the soil together and to confine ploughing to conserving moisture and controlling weeds so that these days such storms are a relatively rare event.

My mother and father both came from local farming families who had pioneered 640 acre Mallee blocks. On my father's side the Glare family (originally spelled Glayre or Gleyre) can trace its roots back to Switzerland in the 1600's and Brabant (now Belgium) in the 1700's. Both those family branches moved to England. The first Glare in Australia, James, came from London as a convict to Port Arthur in 1820 at the age of 19 years. The first Brabyn (originally Brabant), John, in Australia came from Cornwall to Norfolk Island in 1796 as a Captain in the New South Wales Corps. These two families were united with the marriage of a newly emancipated James Glare (convicted in London and sent to Port Arthur in 1820) and Eliza Sophia Mills, the latter descended from John Brabyn, in Launceston in 1830. The couple then moved in 1846 to the Mills family location in Port Fairy, Victoria, as whalers and farmers. John Mills, Sophia's brother, was the harbourmaster at Port Fairy and his cottage is preserved on the wharf there by the National Trust.

> [A history of the Glare family has been published by Marguereta Williams [nee Glare]; *Sans Peur–the origins and history of the Glare family* PenFolk Publishing, Blackburn April 2002 ISBN 1875894276].

> [A history of the Brabyn family *The Life and Times of John Brabyn* was written by Betty McGrath, published 1995 ISBN No. 0 646 25116 3]

My grandfather, John Glare, grandson of James, had brought his family overland by wagon from the Broken Hill Region in outback New South Wales to Hopetoun after a period on the opal fields at White Cliffs. He cleared his

640 acre (259 hectare) Mallee block with one horse and an axe. A smallish wiry man he was extremely tough. Even in his 80's he would fell trees with an axe, cut them up for firewood, and bring them back to the house in a wheelbarrow. As a child I would watch in fascination as he filled his pipe then put his bare hand in the open fire, pulled out a live coal, slowly lit his pipe with the coal while his calluses sizzled and then equally slowly replaced the coal in the fire. Clearly he felt no pain at all so hardened were his hands.

George Glare

My father, born in 1908 at Hopetoun in Victoria, was named Frederick George but always known as George, the seventh child in a family of nine. The family farm could not sustain all the sons so he worked at whatever he could on the land ranging as far afield as the Darling Downs in Queensland droving cattle. When I was born he was 26 and was listed on my birth certificate as a farm labourer although he was actually making his living trapping rabbits.

My mother, Freda Esther Ferguson, born in 1911 at Hopevale near Hopetoun, Victoria, came from a Scottish and Irish heritage. Her father, Benjamin, settled

Freda Esther Glare (nee Ferguson)

his Mallee block after a spell on the opal fields at Coober Pedy in South Australia. Her mother, Janey, was one of 15 children whose father abandoned them and she was taken in by a German farming family. As a result, Mum was Lutheran and I was christened in the Lutheran Church at Hopetoun, a church later burned down by locals during the Second World War as an act of misplaced patriotism. Grandmother Janey died in 1941 on my seventh birthday. Grandfather Benjamin died a few months later.

I have what I think is the only love letter my father wrote in his life, dated 2 May 1931, to my mother when she moved off the farm to become a domestic servant for the Doctor in Hopetoun. She kept it all of her life. He only ever wrote one letter to me and signed it, *'Yours faithfully, George Glare'.*

Mum and Dad were married on 1 February 1934 (easily remembered as 1,2,3,4). They began married life with not much more than a horse and cart and slept under the latter while Dad pursued his rabbit trapping 'profession' at which he was peerless. My arrival 10 months later made that carefree life no longer viable. (Many years later I embarrassed my mother by telling visitors that I was in her wedding photos. It was all above board because there was no photographer in the area when they married and the photographs were taken three months later, by which time I was present although not visible.) They moved into a vacant farmhouse near the Glare farm temporarily then to the original Ferguson house on my grandfather's farm as he was by then in a new farmhouse elsewhere on the property. My earliest memories are of that old house. I started school from there probably at the age of four and a half, riding my tiny 22 inch bicycle about two miles to a one room/one teacher school named Wilhelmina (No.4122) in a remote corner of the Ferguson property. By this time my brother Kelvin (Kel) had been born, just over three years after me. (The land for this school had been gifted by my grandfather and perhaps fifty years later the State Government tried to sell it back to my cousin Lawrence Ferguson who by then owned the farm. The land was absolutely useless to anyone else!). I could read before I went to school but there was very little reading material available so I avidly read the labels on jam jars and the like.

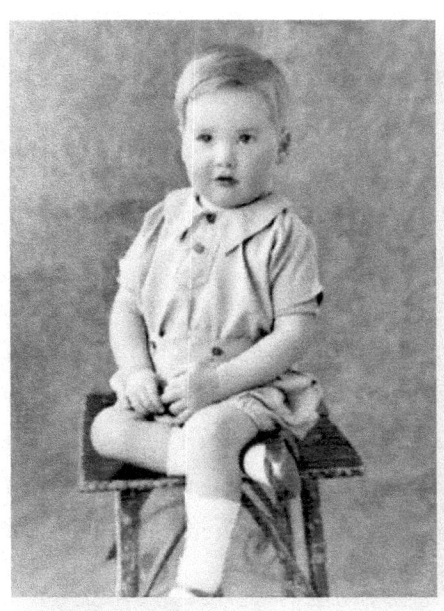
Len at 18 months

Apparently early in my schooling I announced an ambition to be the King or the Prime Minister, neither ever realised although this may have been the first indication of my destiny for a career in public service. I remember my first school day more vividly because another first day student and I were thrown together by the bigger boys and made to fight each other. We scratched and scrabbled for a long time as I recall it before being summoned inside school with the result a nil-all draw.

One day I announced that I did not want to go to school because I was afraid of stray cows across the road—or at least that was the excuse. Dad said nothing but yoked up the horse to the cart, climbed on and started cracking a stockwhip around my ears. I pedalled that bike so fast to school that I think I laid the foundation for a later career in bike racing.

When I was very young, five or six, Dad took me out into the bush and hid from me to see if I would be able to find my way out. My first bushcraft lesson! Fortunately I passed the test. These days when I tell people about that I also tell them that he employed a similar lesson to teach me how to swim by throwing me in the dam. I tell them that the swimming was easy but getting out of the bag was very difficult. I think some believe the latter story too!

Little one teacher country schools were always interesting. They were usually built of weatherboard with a galvanised iron roof and had a water tank filled by rainwater from the roof (see photograph of nearby Yarto school for an example). I remember an early grammar lesson because someone announced that they had seen a porcupine on the way to school (nowadays they are properly known as echidnas but then we used the British term porcupine). The teacher looked around carefully and said, 'It hasn't arrived yet.' Another day the boys caught a frill-necked lizard, brought it to school and amused themselves by getting it to bite on a stick and then tossing it over their heads among the girls.

Once a week, we would all stand lined up and to attention, the Australian flag would be 'run up' the flagpole. The boys would salute and the girls stand to attention. Then we would place our right hand on our heart and recite 'I love God and my country, I honour the flag, I will serve the King and cheerfully obey my parents, teachers and the law'. This of course was King George VI at the time. We also celebrated Empire Day on 24 May and Guy Fawkes Day on 5 November. Colonial affiliation to 'the old country' was still very strong.

Our male teacher had a fondness for galah eggs so his habit was to set us kids the task of robbing nests in hollow trees for eggs which he then boiled in a billy in the open fireplace that was the school's only heating. Much to our amusement he then made his tea in the same boiling water. Our school swimming excursions were to a dam on the Mill's property nearby. Water being very scarce, none of us could swim but our teacher, who came from a wetter area, amazed us with his prowess.

Another excursion was a short walk into the desert to a natural spring which produced pure clear water from the sandy ground. Although the area was very dry and sandy, water could be found beneath the surface in many places if you knew where to dig. A family named Chenoweth established an orchard on sandy soil fed by natural springs near the locality of Yarto. It produced marvellous fruit and the remnants of that abandoned orchard can still be seen today.

About the time I began school World War II broke out and even in this remote corner of Australia there were effects. Every now and then we would save sixpence (5 cents) to buy a postage stamp to affix to a War Savings

Yarto School c.1930

Certificate which went to finance the war effort. A full certificate was worth one whole pound (40 sixpences = $2) and was redeemable at the end of the war, assuming we won. We also made camouflage nets from string for the war effort. I have a vivid memory of a newspaper headline, it must have been in 1940 when Russia was considering whether it would enter the war and on whose side. It read, 'Russia Sits on Fence.' As a simple country boy I recall trying to work out how a country could sit on a fence!

Another effect of the war was that many goods were either unprocurable or could only be bought using coupons from Government supplied ration books. Rationing began in June 1942 and covered items like tea, sugar, petrol and clothing but also extended to milk, eggs, meat and butter which did not affect us on farms. Children didn't get food rations until they were nine years old. Petrol rationing caused many to fit charcoal burning gas producers to their vehicles, either on the side running board that all cars had in those days or the rear bumper, thus replacing petrol. Cars were often started on petrol and then a homemade switch was used to change the fuel from petrol to kerosene, the latter being more readily available on farms. This practice was illegal but rarely detected.

When Japan entered the war and Darwin was bombed, invasion fears ran high. We pupils were required to dig a slit trench in the schoolyard in case of air attack. Just imagine a very remote school with about 10 pupils being worth attacking by anyone. Our digging skills were quite well developed in any case because the outdoor toilets contained cans which we emptied regularly into holes we dug for the purpose. Thank heaven for sandy ground.

Our male teacher, Arthur Doak, left to join the Army and went to Papua New Guinea. He wrote to me regularly and I only wish I had saved the letters. From them I learned about things like 'fuzzy-wuzzy angels', the PNG people who helped our soldiers along the Kokoda Track.

The great event of 1941 was that Dad secured a job operating a large farm for Sir Louis Bussau who was Victoria's Agent-General in London. It was two miles from where we were then living. We went to inspect our new home and found only a single room hut constructed of narrow gauge corrugated iron, without any ceiling or wall linings and with a small one-fire wood stove at the western end. You can imagine how hot that was in summer and how cold in winter. The former caretaker, Tom O'Brien, had been a single man. There wasn't even a toilet, just a tree branch between two tree forks. Our first task was to bury the mess.

Dad built two main rooms and two smaller rooms, from mostly second hand materials, on the southern side of the existing hut which became our kitchen. The two sections were connected by a small wooden deck that created a breezeway. Only the two front rooms had small glass windows. The other rooms had corrugated iron flaps that could be raised and propped open with a stick. An outdoor toilet was constructed about 100 yards from the house and a straw-roofed lean-to with a dirt floor became the laundry. Mum swept that dirt floor almost every day. A wood-fired copper stood outside the laundry in the open air and it was there that Mum did the washing. She also made her own soap in the copper from caustic soda and boiled down animal fat. Occasionally the copper served for cooking yabbies as well. There was no bathroom. Saturday was bath night and, as water was very scarce, we all went

Site of our farmhouse on the Bussau property
(Photo courtesy of Kelvin Glare)

through the same hip bath in the kitchen, contrary to oral tradition, from youngest to oldest. With this system it wasn't a case of throwing the baby out with the bathwater, although Dad encountered some very dubious water when his turn came.

My younger brother Kel and I walked about two miles each way to school across sandy paddocks. This short-cut meant traversing the Surridge property on the other side of what was then the Hopetoun-Patchewollock road. We necessarily went through the Surridge houseyard and often attracted the attention of Mrs Surridge who was something of a harridan. Because of her hair colour, her husband Arthur called her 'The Red Light of Ireland.' Our father had been deemed medically unfit for active war service but Mrs Surridge's eldest son, Mick, had been called up and later died when the hospital ship on which he was serving as a medical orderly was sunk. Mrs Surridge often pursued us through the houseyard with such comments as, 'Poor little boys; your father won't fight in the war!' One day the two younger Surridge boys, Brian and Terry, who were older than me, put me on top of their chestnut hack (Jean) bareback and facing backwards and then cracked the horse with a stockwhip. It took off across the paddock with me holding on to the tail for dear life. Fortunately, I didn't fall off and the horse eventually tired.

Another horse adventure came about because, in those days, routine warnings such as 'Do Not Try This At Home' were not given. I went to the circus and saw trick riders standing on horseback while sending their steeds at some speed around the circus ring. At home I cautiously stood on the hind quarters of the horse, then started it walking. That was quite easy so I increased the speed to a trot. Still no problem. Unfortunately, the canter brought me undone and I crashed, hurting mainly my pride.

Len and Kel on the farm 1940

By the end of my Grade 4 Kel and I came to constitute 50% of the school pupil population and

Wilhelmina school was closed. (It wasn't the last we saw of it because it was transported physically into Hopetoun where it became a freestanding part of the Higher Elementary School). We then went to a 'big' school, Wathe, which had 14 pupils and one teacher (Ellie Wilkinson) who boarded at our farm. We drove the eight miles each way in a horse-drawn cart picking up some other kids along the way. The horse spent its days feeding from a nosebag of chaff in the shade of a tree. Wathe school went only to Grade 6. Delegation by the teacher saw me, while nominally in Grade 5, teaching the first four grades most of the time. Strangely perhaps, I never rated very well in terms of end of year marks; she didn't like me and the feeling was mutual. One day we were caught in a Mallee dust storm shortly after leaving school for home. We sheltered down in the cart under wheat bags to protect us from choking dust and flying debris while the horse that we could not even see from the cart found its way home.

Life on the farm was spartan in the extreme but I never felt deprived. I think that I had the most wonderful childhood despite never owning a bought toy. We played with what we made. We had no motor car until I was nine and trips to Hopetoun (14 kilometres away) for shopping necessitated either a long drive in the horse-drawn cart or hitchhiking on the tray back of a neighbour's truck after walking from the farm to the road. Friday was market day in Hopetoun. If we went by horse and cart there were stalls available for the horse either behind the grocery store or behind the pub. We tended to shop in bulk for staple items that would keep for long periods to avoid trips to town. There was no refrigeration but only a Coolgardie safe which was a small home-made cupboard the walls of which were charcoal contained by wire netting. The safe was kept outside. Cooling came from hessian draped over its exterior with the bottom edges trailing in a water tray. The water percolated up the hessian and the breeze through the wet hessian provided the cooling. It sounds primitive and it was but it was remarkably effective.

Because of these infrequent trips to town for supplies, we carefully rationed ourselves. This led to a young Kel one day telling Dad's brother

Uncle Jack who was visiting, 'Go easy on the tomato sauce. It has to last until Friday.'

There was no electricity and no running water in the house. We had a car battery operated Chrysler radio in a tall cabinet, looking like a piece of furniture. Our lighting was by kerosene lamps and lanterns. More affluent households than ours used kerosene lamps with mantles made of fibre that burned with an incandescent glow and gave off very white light. Our drinking water came from a 1,000 gallon tank which was filled by rainwater collected from the house roof. With such a dry climate, extreme frugality with water was essential. Water for bathing and washing clothes came from a dam not far from the house and was brought up in a rusty 44 gallon drum lashed to a forked tree branch and dragged by a horse. That water was far from drinkable; it smelt terrible and I don't know how Mum ever got the clothes clean, even with boiling everything. Once I was on foot without water far from home and desperately thirsty but the nearest dam, besides containing poor quality water, had dead sheep in it. I drank it anyway (from the far end of the dam) and it didn't taste too bad. The blanket for my bed was three wheat bags sewn together lengthwise. It was very warm and at least the bags were new at first.

Despite the dryness of the climate and the sandy soil, one day brought a cloudburst over the slight hill just above the house. Water cascaded down the slope and through the houseyard at a depth of 100 millimetres carrying straw and other rubbish before it. It was a short-lived sight that I never saw again.

The dust storms would blow brambles against the wire netting houseyard fence then drift sand would be caught by the brambles. At the end of a dust storm it often required a horse-drawn scoop to dig the fence out again. About 1.5 metres high, the fence would be completely covered by sand in an hour.

We had a telephone attached to a party line emanating from the telephone exchange in Hopetoun with about eight farmhouses connected to it. Power for the line came from two 6 volt batteries installed in each phone on the party line. To call someone it was necessary to turn the magneto hand ringing device to generate 50 volts to create a letter in Morse code. The line number was 84 and our location was 'K' so that if someone gave a long-short-long ring we knew it was for us and we answered. If we wanted to call my grandparents on the same line we gave 'short-short-short' representing the letter 'S'. To call the Hopetoun telephone exchange it was one long ring. To call someone on another line required getting the telephonist at the exchange to answer when the manual shutter on the 84 line fell down under vibration from the ring tone, ascertain who we wanted and then connect through the switchboard (by a cord terminating in a plug) through a jack system our line to whatever other line we were seeking. A constant temptation was for others on the party line to eavesdrop and each additional party on the line lowered the power level so that it became difficult to hear. My father used the tactic of saying, 'Get off the line Mrs Surridge' and that was effective. She could not object without confessing that she had been listening.

Early party line telephone LM Ericsson 121 magneto wall unit manufactured in Sweden in 1913.
Photo courtesy of Des Walsh

In the earlier years the Mallee trees that had been rolled flat to clear the land put forth shoots from the buried stumps and it was the task of all male members of the family to cut these shoots with a scythe on a long handle so as to prevent the paddocks being overrun by trees again. The stump-jump plough, invented in South Australia in 1876, allowed paddocks to be cultivated by jumping the ploughshares over stump obstructions rather than being caught behind them. Mallee stumps were deep-rooted and horse-drawn ploughs could not easily remove them. Cutting Mallee shoots was hard and tedious labour. In later years improved machinery allowed stumps to be lifted out so that shoot cutting was no longer required.

The farm was devoted primarily to sheep and wheat. As the oldest son, on arrival home from school each day it was my task to climb on a horse and 'go round' the sheep. This was for the purpose of locating any that were 'down', that is, sick or fly-struck by blowflies. Sometimes sheep became stuck in the mud at the edge of dams and would become too weak to extricate themselves. Saddles were too expensive to be wasted on kids so almost all of my riding was bareback.

Two very different horses were my usual mounts. One was Sylvie, a quarter-draught who was not tall and quite broad across the beam. Sitting on her bareback was not easy with legs not long enough to go round the curve. The other was a former trotter called Glen Moonee. He was 17 hands tall and posed a different problem. Without a saddle to climb up on, I would take him near a fence, climb up on the fence and launch myself onto his back. However, he was quite cunning and would wait until I launched myself before taking a couple of sideways steps so that I would land on the ground instead of his back. It often took half a dozen attempts before I was safely mounted.

Stump-jump plough.
Wikipedia

My grandfather Ben Ferguson had a magnificent stable of draught horses and from about five years of age I had the wonderful experience of driving a fifteen horse team pulling the farm machinery. There were at that stage very few tractors in the area. Each day on his farm started with preparing the horses and each day finished with grooming, feeding and watering them. The smell of steaming horses was pervasive in the colder weather. I got a ride on the back of one of the draught horses to and from the paddock.

The work day was sunrise to sunset. Grain from the wheat harvest was put into individual wheat bags each filled bag containing 3 bushels and weighing 180 pounds (81 kilograms). The bags were stacked upright, with the tops open, in groups awaiting top-up filling and sewing. Tight filling was achieved by inserting a long metal funnel with a hopper at the top into the loosely filled bag of wheat, filling the hopper with grain and then moving the funnel up and down to force grain from the hopper into the bag until it was tightly packed. The tops of the bags were then hand sewn with a needle and twine,

Draught horses.
Source Luvyalockyer.com.au

the bags loaded onto a horse-drawn wagon and taken to the nearest railway siding. A grip on the smooth tightly-filled bags was aided by bag hooks, two curved hooks mounted on a wooden handle. One of my childhood pleasures was to ride on top of the bags while they were delivered to the railway siding.

A particular piece of magic was the reaper and binder machine which was used to cut hay from oats. As the wheels of the machine turned while being dragged along by the horses, gears from the wheels operated a saw-like blade over a wide comb to cut off the oat stalks near the ground. A mechanical arm then gathered the cut stalks into bundles where an ingenious mechanical piece tied twine around them and cut it off. The bundles, called sheaves, were then mechanically ejected from the machine by a swinging arm and were gathered by hand to be placed, heads of grain uppermost, in groups resembling Indian tepees. The groups were called stooks. From there the sheaves were heaved individually with a pitchfork by a man at ground level up onto the wagon where another man built up the load in overlapping layers so that it held together for its journey back to the house paddock. Once there, the sheaves were built into a haystack so well constructed that it held itself together and the outer layer repelled water. The hay was used in part for feeding stock but it was also fed through a chaffcutter which turned it into fine particles that were sent up through an elevator into the chaffhouse. The chaff was used to feed the horses. I still remember the wonderful aroma of newly-mown hay.

A humorous incident occurred once when a snake remained unseen in a sheaf of hay and was pitchforked up to the man on top of the wagon. He promptly stepped straight off the top of the load and landed on the ground more than five metres below on his feet, surprisingly uninjured.

Haystack building from wagon.
Source: Bytes

Our diet was largely made up of things that we could kill or grow. Rabbits were plentiful, indeed in plague proportions, and were a staple. Poultry we kept in large numbers, about 70 fowl and 20 ducks at a time, so eggs and what is now called chicken formed a large part of our diet. Chicken then meant a small juvenile bird and we tended to kill and eat only the

Haystack with mouse guard around it.
Source: Bytes

old 'chooks' who were past their egg laying prime. Similarly, although we ran about 1,000 sheep at a time we did not kill lambs because they fetched the best market price and we ate a lot of very mature mutton which we slaughtered and dressed ourselves. One of our simple country pleasures was to take the extracted bladders from the dressed sheep, inflate them and use them for footballs. The area had cattle only for milking so beef was not part of our diet. My mother always threatened to write a cookbook entitled '1001 Ways to Cook Rabbit.' Perhaps this is why, today, I cannot eat rabbit or chicken.

Daily milking of the cow provided us with milk, cream and butter. Usually the kids milked the cow, by hand of course, and occasionally we would squeeze some of the warm milk straight from the cow into our mouths. No such thing as pasteurisation. Nowadays you will pay a lot of money for unprocessed milk. We ran some of the milk through a hand operated separator to gather the cream and then churned that cream by hand until it became butter. The butter was formed into blocks by patting it with wooden paddles. The home-made butter contained no salt and when I first tasted butter from the shop I found it very unpalatable.

Mum made bread every two or three days. The hand worked dough was placed in high loaf tins and cooked in the wood fire oven. The smell and taste of that fresh baked bread is with me even today. A typical packed lunch for school contained fresh bread spread with lard. Not exactly a recommended diet these days. Because our diet contained few green vegetables for most of the year, we often suffered from boils and carbuncles which were very painful and uncomfortable.

Clothes and linen were ironed with flat irons heated on top of the wood fire stove. The clothes we wore were very basic and children didn't have the luxury of underwear. Footwear for all occasions was boots, usually the same pair for everything. For school football matches we tacked leather bars across the soles temporarily to act as primitive stops. Because of the climate we did wear hats outdoors otherwise our melanoma problems would have been much greater in later life.

My second brother, Rob, was born two days after my birthday in December 1942. While Mum was in hospital Dad tried his hand at baking his first ever cake. He omitted the bicarbonate of soda (self-raising flour had been invented in 1845 but had not yet reached us) and the cake emerged flatter than a pancake. Even the farm dogs would not eat it. No more cake making!

When Rob was about two years old I was driving the gig, a light horse-drawn cart with two wheels and a high superstructure, with Rob sitting between Kel and me. The right wheel hit a hidden stump and propelled Kel over the side and under the left wheel which went over his stomach. I caught Rob by the pants or he would have followed. Kel got up saying, 'I can see blobs of fire'. I think that he still blames me for his health problems, his hiatus hernia in particular.

We used kerosene as a panacea. Dad was straining a fence and the wire broke and went straight through the palm of his hand and out the other side. He poured kerosene through it and no infection ensued. Rob put a garden fork through his foot and pinned himself to the ground. Mum stood on his foot, pulled the fork out and poured kerosene in the wound. When we had a sore throat it was a teaspoon of sugar soaked with a few drops of kerosene. Harsh but effective.

In 1944 when I was nine we acquired a motor car. It was a 1927 Chevrolet National and I immediately learned to drive—a necessity for a farm boy. I drove everywhere on the farm and on the roads as well. I had driven a tractor from much earlier and a large part of my role on the farm was tractor driving. The then undiagnosed illness which had kept my father out of the war sometimes rendered him physically unable to drive the tractor. During harvest the problem was that I was not yet strong enough to lift the full bags of wheat from the harvester into the stacks in the paddock awaiting collection. Dad would lie in the shade of the bags and when I periodically pulled in to empty the hopper of grain he would summon the strength to lift the bags into place and then collapse again. Grain collection has now

1927 Chevrolet National.
Source: Vintage Motor Club

become mechanised so that there is little labour in it today. The price I paid for all of this tractor work, done without the shelter of a cabin or any ear protection, has been deafness in later life caused by that acoustic trauma in my early years.

Our farm was the turning point for RAAF fighter planes on training runs from the air base at Nhill. Sometimes they would practise strafing runs on our horse and cart. We got a very close look at them.

I have a clear memory of learning of the end of the World War II on VP day (Victory in the Pacific) also known as VJ day (Victory over Japan) on 15 August 1945. Dad and I had just returned to the house in the cart, tied up the horse outside, when Mum came rushing out to tell us that she had heard the announcement by Prime Minister Chifley on the radio.

One compensation for living remotely was that, because of the total absence of ambient light, the night sky was absolutely brilliant. I would lie on my back in the green wheat crop and look at the stars that seemed close enough to touch.

Making Ends Meet

Dad got only two pounds ($4) a week for working the farm so he supplemented his income by any means possible. The Mallee region was then serviced by a system of channels that brought water from the Grampians Mountains far to the south. These channels were gravity fed and created an amazing network to fill the dams that were dug on each property. Once a year the water came up and the dams near the channel would be filled progressively by manually turning the water into them through drains leading off the channels. Because the land was sandy, drift sand tended to block the channels and each year sub-contractors were engaged to clean them out using horse-drawn scoops just before the water was due to arrive. The scoops were of metal with skids beneath to slide over the soil. Scoops had two long wooden handles to control manually the depth of cut into the soil. When shifted below their normal housing location, the handles enabled the scoop to be lifted and overturned on the channel banks thus emptying the collected soil. This meant driving the horses backwards and forwards at right angles to the channel and clearing it a scoop width at a time. As the scoops were only about 3 metres wide it was a tedious business. My father was one of the sub-contractors and, to eliminate travel time, he camped in a tent with a group of others near the leading edge of each day's clearance.

These were gold rush style low tents of canvas with no floor. A sheet of canvas called a fly was suspended above the tent to make it rainproof. As a child I found camping out fascinating, sitting round the campfire at night listening to the men talking. The night sky was usually clear; to quote Banjo Paterson's *Clancy of the Overflow*, 'And at night the wond'rous glory of the everlasting stars'. In recent years the entire open channel system has been replaced by PVC pipes with huge savings in water from eliminating seepage and evaporation. Reportedly, only 6% of the water formerly used is now required.

Of course there was no exogenous entertainment on the channel camp, not even a radio. Campfire conversations were vigorous and full of humour and I listened avidly. I recall the men around the campfire one night kidding an older man, Tom Holland, that the Government was about to regulate sex in marriage as part of the war effort. He was quite outraged and yelled, 'No bloody Government is going to stop Mum and me having our two a week.'

Once Dad became sick while on the channels and the others placed him in an iron scoop, dragged directly over the ground by horses, to get him back to camp. It is a wonder that the ride didn't kill him.

I recall Dad being sick on another occasion when he drove the horse and cart back to the house then promptly fell on his face on the ground from the full height of the cart. Mum and I dragged him onto a bed. Young Rob came in, took one look at him, and announced quite impassively, 'He's dead!' Fortunately he wasn't.

Our main supplementary income came from rabbits which were perpetually in plague proportions. Trapping rabbits, poisoning rabbits, netting them with the aid of ferrets and, more expensively, shooting them. My father, frugal by necessity and habit, often killed a rabbit by throwing a trap hammer or tyre lever at it rather than waste an expensive bullet. His aim was unerring.

Trapping entailed setting a number of traps, perhaps two or three hundred, in the late afternoon. The most common brand of traps was Lane

Ace; they had an ace of spades embossed on the tongue. Using our knowledge of rabbit habits and the terrain, we would excavate a shallow scrape in their traffic paths with the blade side of a trap hammer, place the trap in the scrape, depress the trap spring and set the trigger over it with a metal flap engaging the metal tongue to hold it down. A small square of newspaper would then be placed over the tongue so that sand would not fall underneath it and prevent the tongue from being depressed by the weight of the rabbit. The trap itself was tethered in the ground by a steel peg attached to a light chain. The whole arrangement was disguised with a thin layer of sandy soil. When the rabbit stepped on the tongue it depressed, releasing the spring and catching the rabbit by the leg in the steel jaws. Occasionally a fox would step on a trap and, being stronger than a rabbit, pull out the peg and drag the trap away so that we needed to follow the trail to recover the trap. Releasing the fox could be hazardous as they did not react well to people. There were still a few dingo traps around but dingoes in the area had been eradicated by then.

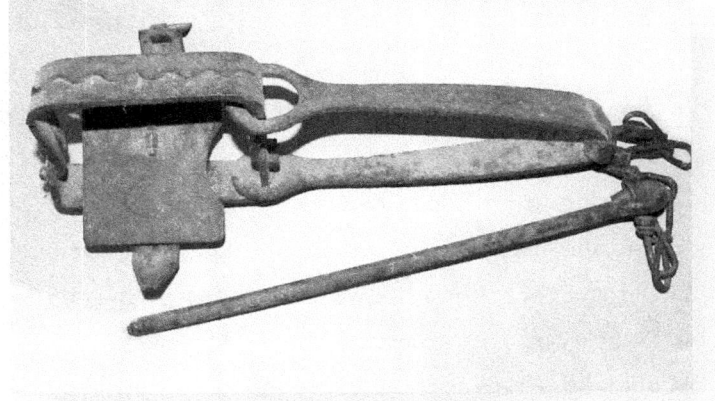

Rabbit trap made by Henry Lane (Australia) Ltd, 1935—1960.
Powerhouse Collection

We would 'go round the traps' for the first time between midnight and 2am, take the rabbits out of the traps, quickly break their necks and place the carcases in bags then reset the traps. The second round of the traps was conducted at daybreak before birds could attack the trapped rabbits. Early in the morning we would then gut the rabbits leaving the skins on, cut slits in one hind leg so that the other leg could be passed through the slit and hang them by the crossed legs over a sturdy stick in pairs. The paired rabbits were then placed in a roadside tree and covered with hessian to keep off flies and await collection by the rabbit freezer van. I would not have liked to eat those rabbits by the time they got to the cities!

Another income source was farmers who would pay to have the rabbit population on their properties reduced. In these cases we dug Scotch Thistle roots, cut them into bait lengths, and rolled them in vanilla, cornflour and strychnine. In the paddocks we would then plough an irregular shallow single furrow and distribute the baits along the length of the furrow. The rabbits were attracted to the furrow and then discovered and ate the baits. Within a few seconds they were dead from heart failure and at daybreak we would collect the carcasses in the horse-drawn cart. Because of the poison they were useless for the table but the skins were valuable for such things as making felt hats (which all men then wore, city or country). One morning I remember well because my father and I, with the help of Uncle Joe and one or two others, skinned 1,040 rabbits. The number was so great that there were 27 yellow rabbits among them as well as black and piebald ones. The carcasses then had to be buried and the skins taken home, stretched over lengths of fencing wire shaped like a hairpin and dried by the sun while leaning against the sheepyard fences. A dried rabbit skin is not much heavier than a small bunch of feathers but we often had enough to fill wool bales ready for sale at about sixpence a pound.

One unpleasant side effect of collecting rabbits in the cart was that we necessarily sat on top of them to ride home. Each night Mum would manually pick all the rabbit fleas from my body before I went to bed. Only a mother would do that.

One thing that still puzzles me is that Dad mixed those strychnine baits with his bare hands and must have absorbed some through his skin without apparent effect. I have heard that strychnine was sometimes used to treat heart conditions.

Ferreting was fun. My Uncle Joe Ferguson kept 25 to 30 ferrets in a pit. When he wanted to go ferreting he would put me in the pit to hand up ferrets to him. For some reason they would bite him with their very sharp teeth if he put his hand in but, when I was very young, they didn't bite me. How Joe first discovered this still troubles me a little. (A ferret bite is not funny because their sharp teeth lock on and it is very difficult to get them to let go). The ferret box and nets were then transported to a rabbit warren and nets placed over the mouths of burrows. The ferret was inserted and chased the rabbits out into the nets where we could capture them. Sometimes a ferret would corner a rabbit or rabbit kittens underground, kill them and then feast and not come out. It was then necessary to set a fire at the mouth of the burrow to smoke the ferret out. One day a ferret encountered a fox within a burrow and from the noise we knew what was going on. Joe armed himself with a heavy branch, stood astride the burrow and waited for the fox to appear. Unfortunately, the ferret appeared first being chased by the fox and Joe reflexively brought down the branch on the poor ferret while the fox escaped between his legs. I was highly amused but he wasn't and, being excitable by nature, his language with quite inventive.

Another method of generating extra income was to tour the desert edges in a horse-drawn cart looking for sheep that had wandered in there and perished. We would pluck the wool from the carcases and put it in the cart, again, sitting on top of the load. At home we would spread the rotting wool out on wire netting suspended between trees to allow the sun to kill off the maggots and the dirt and debris to fall out. This wool was eventually sold for such things as making carpets.

Dad also did some contract fencing for farmers. This entailed cutting the fence posts from live trees with an axe, digging postholes by hand, boring holes in the posts, passing wires through the posts and intermediate wooden spacers called droppers, then using a strainer to tighten the wires. The top wire was invariably barbed wire.

The neighbouring Malcolm brothers once engaged me to stand behind their harvester in a cocky chaff carrier, a cage on wheels, and rake the waste debris raining down overhead from harvesting process back in the carrier so that more could come down. I was promised a pound a week for this filthy job where I was protected only by Perspex goggles but I never saw the money. In the interest of neighbourly relations Dad didn't make a fuss. The injustice of this rankled with me for many years.

Diversions

A side effect of shooting from an early age was that I became an excellent shot as did my brothers. Dad, a good teacher but hard taskmaster, insisted that I practice shooting the heads off horizontal matches with .22 calibre rifle at a range of about the length of a cricket pitch. This was more difficult than shooting at vertical matches because it is easier to track up and down a vertical target. The corollary of this training was that, when I entered the RAAF for national service, the rifle shooting part was very easy for me. A target the size of a barn! How could anyone miss? Shooting did have its hazards. One day my younger brother Rob was following in single file behind me when we came upon a snake. I raised my rifle, took aim and 'bang', the snake's head was shot off. From behind me came Rob's excited cry, '*Good shot Len*'. The only problem was that I hadn't fired. In his excitement Rob fired past me without even realising he had pulled the trigger. After that he led the way!

Our farmhouse was a regular Sunday gathering place particularly for the young men in the area. Entertainment consisted of impromptu rodeos, cricket matches and home-grown Olympic Games. One rodeo event was for one of the young men to ride a steer bareback while it was restrained from running too far by a rope. I recall Dad being pulled off his feet by the steer and dragged face first through a cowpat. A great deal of laughter accompanied all of these games. How Mum managed to feed all these people never ceased to amaze me. Her baking ability was legendary.

Card playing and draughts were frequent pastimes. When I was eight, Dad challenged an elderly neighbour, Sam Mill, to play draughts against me. I won and Dad cackled all the way home. Occasionally there would be a barn dance, sometimes on roller skates. At one of these my father picked up a concertina and played with the band all night. I had never seen him touch one before.

Before my Uncle Wal Ferguson and his sister Auntie Hilda married sister and brother Gladys and Gordon Mitchell in a double ceremony, there was a 'tin-kettling' at the Malcolm farm. This consisted of a procession of people beating kettles, pots and pans or anything else they could find to make a lot of noise. The procession concluded at the barn for a supper and dance and the giving of presents. I don't think that this piece of early Australian country ritual has survived to modern times.

The regular visits of Indian hawkers to the farm were a source of interest and delight for the younger members of the family. These hawkers had covered wagons drawn by a single horse. The wagons were laden with household goods of every description—pots, pans, kitchen utensils, needle and thread, material for dressmaking and so on. The farm women relied heavily on these hawkers who were all Sikhs and, of course, wore turbans. As with all Sikhs their surname was Singh. One that I recall was named Nuttah Singh. Our farm was their regular overnight camp in the area and at night we children were drawn by the magic of their campfires and the exotic smell of curry. They were extremely sociable and welcomed us to sit with them. We were always sorry to see them leave next day.

Indian hawker and farmer on a farm at Carapook, Victoria, 1924.
Image: Arthur Pearce Museum Victoria Collection

Once a year we put the sheep through a chemical dip to destroy vermin. The dip was a narrow concrete tub with a slope at the beginning. The sheep would be brought through a wooden fenced race, stand on the slippery down slope of the dip, slide into the main body of it and then swim to the other end to get out. On their way down we used a wooden T-bar to push their heads under the surface to make sure they were properly immersed. At the end of the day's work the dogs usually got a dip too. Periodically we would drive a mob of sheep to town for sale helped by the sheepdogs. Our reward on the home journey in the cart was a snack of hot pigs' trotters in a brown paper bag. (We had never heard of cholesterol).

Shearing of the sheep was also an annual event. In the early days hand shears were used but these later were replaced by mechanical clippers powered through flexible links by a stationary motor. My hands weren't strong enough to operate hand shears on grown sheep but I got to 'crutch' lambs, that is, clip the dung matted areas around their tails. I can still smell the mixed lanolin and sheep manure of the sheds.

Dad trained his own sheepdogs and some of them were quite marvellous. His favourite was called Glen and there wasn't much that dog could not understand. Dad would speak to him in a conversational manner and give him instructions, for example, *'Bring home those rams from the top paddock'*. The dog would cut the rams out of the flock without further help or instruction and bring them home. He also trained Glen in a kind of circus act through an obstacle course circumnavigating the house. Dad's methods were sometimes harsh. If a dog ran away and wouldn't come back when called he would fire a rifle shot over its head. The dog then faced a choice of coming back or taking the next bullet. Dad was offered huge amounts of money for Glen but would never sell him.

Every few years the area was visited with a mouse plague. Under favourable breeding conditions mice bred in plague proportions and infested everything. Driving at night was like driving through water as the waves of mice spread in front of the car. Cats ran away from the mice, being overwhelmed by sheer numbers. Babies had to be protected carefully because mice would nibble them. Mice nested in beds and in a very short space of time would create an unbelievable mess. One method used to try to keep the numbers down was to place greased wire across the top of 44 gallon drums containing water making sure that the mice had some means of climbing to the top. The mice would slip from the wire and drown and huge numbers of them were removed each morning. The fowl gorged themselves on mice and when we killed one it would contain quantities of semi-digested mice, another reason for me not to eat chicken. These plagues ended very abruptly and naturally through over-breeding and changing weather conditions.

Once I was driving the tractor several miles from the house when I unwittingly ran over the tail of a six foot (two metre) long brown snake which reared up and bit me on the shin. Brown snakes are very deadly. After despatching the snake with a chain, I drove the tractor back to the house—a slow trip without a road gear on the tractor. Mum could not drive so she called Uncle Joe to come and drive me to the Doctor. She telephoned the Doctor to warn him and he gave instructions for Joe to call at the Pharmacy to pick up anti-venine and then meet him at the hospital. By the time all of this happened it was about an hour and a half from when I was bitten before I got the antidote. However, I had no ill-effects and ran in the school sports the next day after overnighting in hospital. At the time I expected to die but I think that, being a skinny kid and struck on the shinbone, very little venom was actually injected.

The channels bringing water to the farms also brought some fish to the dams. Sometimes they prospered and we would go to a farm dam as a kind of picnic to net fish, mostly redfin. Dad had made a long flat-topped four-wheel trailer drawn by a single horse. The front wheels and shafts were mounted on a turntable because the trailer was too long to turn otherwise. The neighbours would gather at our place with their picnic lunches, then sit on the trailer dangling their legs over the side while we rode to the fishing site. The sheepdogs rode with their hind legs on the trailer and their front legs on the narrow shafts. Fish was an unusual temporary addition to our diet. Yabbies, (small freshwater crayfish), were constantly in the dams and delicious to eat. The advent of pipes to replace channels, mentioned earlier, has eliminated most of the dams and hence most of the yabbies.

Somewhere I learned a party trick with yabbies that has amused my children and grandchildren over the years. I take the yabbies from the net and 'hypnotise' them by standing them on their pointy noses and gently rubbing the curve of the shells over the tail end. After a minute or so I release them and they stand perfectly still on their noses. I like to line up 20 or so of them. After several minutes they gradually recover, fall back to the ground and move naturally again. I don't know why it works.

Picnic races at Patchewollock were an annual event. Uncle Joe had racehorses and entered his best one each year. Being skinny and light, I rode his horses unless they were not properly broken. Only three or four horses competed in each race. Around the back of the racecourse the track went through a stand of native pine and strange things seemed to happen out of sight of the stewards and spectators. I remember once after the races Joe went back to the local pub and I tagged along. Wandering through the hotel, never having been in one before, I found a bathroom with running water. I was hot and dusty so I ran a bath and climbed in; no one disturbed me.

School picnics were entertaining. Foot racing, bag racing (hopping along inside wheat bags), sheaf tossing (over a pole vault type bar), long jump, high jump and catching the greased pig were some of the events.

My first sight of the sea occurred after harvest in the late summer of 1942. We went to Portland on the south-western coast of Victoria for a holiday, the only one I can recall. We travelled by train and changed trains at Ballarat where we had some hours to kill and I saw my first tram and had my first tram ride, in Lydiard Street I think. There was a large grass fire burning for miles beside the railway line between Ballarat and Portland. On arriving at Portland in the late evening we ate at a cafe and I recall being so tired that I went to sleep standing up leaning against the cafe wall and slid to the floor. Of course the seaside was beyond my imaginings.

These were just some of our diversions. A major one occurred in 1944 when I was sent to the Lord Mayor's holiday camp for underprivileged children at Mt Martha on the Mornington Peninsular south of Melbourne. The camp was in a largely disused Army base which by that time housed only Italian prisoners-of-war. There were no fences and no guards that I could see. The Italian prisoners did not want to escape and roamed around quite freely. The Navy provided an excursion for us on H.M.A.S. Ararat, a corvette, in Westernport Bay out of Flinders Naval Base. The highlight for me was being given the wheel to steer the ship. After driving ponderous tractors I was not ready for the extreme responsiveness of the corvette and swung the wheel too enthusiastically. It took some time for the cook to forgive me for upsetting his galley.

So much of my life has been influenced by my farm upbringing. Work ethic, self-reliance and self-confidence all were imbued then. Spending so much time in physical activity shaped my body and gave me a basis for lifelong fitness.

To paraphrase *Clancy of the Overflow*, 'For the country life has pleasures that the townsfolk never know.'

At the end of 1945 I completed Grade 6 and the problem was how to get to High School. The nearest school offering Grades above 6 was Hopetoun Higher Elementary but there was no means of getting to school each day. The temporary solution was for Kel and me to board with an aunt, my mother's older sister Dorrie, in Sea Lake about 30 miles from home. Her husband was a butcher. After about three months we moved back to Hopetoun to be closer to our parents' farm and boarded Monday to Friday with Dad's youngest sister, Auntie Myrtle. She was a very rough and ready woman but kind-hearted. The next year a school bus began to run from our neighbourhood to Hopetoun and we moved back to the farm full-time again. This bus was an Army surplus utility truck with a canopy on the back. The seating was two long wooden stools arranged on either side of the truck but not secured to the floor nor were the passengers secured in any way. What a reaction that arrangement would attract these days.

Part Two
Transition From the Farm

Town Life

In early 1947 Sir Louis sold the farm. He offered it to us but Dad would not borrow money to finance it and so we left the farm and moved into Hopetoun. We bought a very old house at 27 Dennys Street. It had served variously as a hospital, a police station and a clergyman's residence. One elderly lady gleefully pointed out to us where coffins had rested in our lounge room before funerals. The house was clad internally and externally with pressed metal and had the usual corrugated iron roof. The external design imitated brick with raised portions of metal originally painted white to look like grouting, the remainder painted red. The interior had various decorative designs pressed into the metal. This remained the family home until Kel and I demolished it about 2003 after Mum had gone into the retirement village. We sold the materials from the demolition and found that the pressed metal had become quite valuable. My son Travis, who is a talented painter, did an oil painting of the house before its demolition and that has pride of place in my home today. When Kel and I were about to drop the last of the walls we got Mum from the retirement home in her wheelchair so that she could say goodbye to the old house and perhaps feel some form of closure. She watched quite unemotionally and then said, *'Thanks for doing that. I think I will go back to the village now.'* We should have known that she was strong and practical and would move on without a second thought.

Family House at 27 Dennys Street, Hopetoun.
Painting by Travis Glare

Dad initially got a job as a railway line maintenance worker and serviced the 30 miles or so of line between Hopetoun and Patchewollock. Except during the harvest season, trains continued on to Patchewollock only on Saturday nights. The main issue in track maintenance was clearing drift sand from the line. I asked Dad how he got a job on the railways as he was colour blind. He said it was easy; the red signal was always the one on top. In school holidays I would hitch a ride on the motorised railway tricycle, get off in the middle of the desert with my rifle in the morning, and meet the trike again on the way home in the late afternoon. I never saw another human being while in the desert on these outings.

Hopetoun at that time had a population of 1,500 which had about halved by 2014. It had been established by pastoralist Peter McGinnis at Lake Corrong on Yarriambiack Creek in 1846 with a huge holding of 433,700 acres (177,512 hectares). Corrong Station was renamed Hopetoun in 1890 in honour of a visit by Lord Hopetoun as Governor of Victoria. In 1947 it was a thriving rural centre with two hotels, two banks, three butchers, two grocers and a higher elementary school.

My brothers and I attended the Higher Elementary School; I began there about one third of the way through First Form or what is now Year 7. Attending a much larger school was a new experience. Thanks to an excellent memory, I was a good scholar always finishing in the top three in class without much effort or study. I secured part-time jobs such as a nightly paper round covering half the town. The papers did not arrive by train from Melbourne until the evening so morning papers were delivered in the evening. The main paper read by locals was the Melbourne Sun and I delivered an average of 300 of these by bicycle each day. Other Melbourne newspapers and periodicals were also delivered with a loud cry of 'Paperoooo'. Six days a week earned me 5 shillings (50 cents). My paper boy predecessors told me that during the war, on the rare occasions American servicemen ventured into the town, it was a bonanza. Having a lot of money by our standards, they liked to show off by buying the whole contents of the paper boy's bag. Of course they didn't actually want the papers so the boys would then go on and deliver them as usual. I worked from time to time in the newsagency on counter sales and also delivering groceries and worked in a butcher shop as delivery boy and general hand. Sausage making and injecting corned beef with brine I particularly enjoyed.

An occasional job was at the local greyhound 'Plumpton' or coursing ground. There a live hare was released to be chased by a pair of greyhounds over a course about one kilometre long. The dogs were released by a man called a 'slipper' who restrained the pair on a single leash with two collars and then released the collars simultaneously when the hare had a sufficient head start. As the leading dog reached it, the hare would turn sharply and the dog that caused it to turn would be awarded one point by the judge. Each time it was turned the dog responsible got a point. If a dog went past the other dog on the outer circle, that is the longest arc, and turned the hare it got a bonus point for a 'go by'. On the rare occasions that the dogs actually caught a hare the victorious dog was awarded points for a kill. Eventually the hare would usually reach the end of the course and escape under a barrier so that the dogs could not follow. It lived to race another day. Bookmakers were plentiful and betting vigorous.

My first job at the Plumpton was to lie down alongside the race where the hare first emerged and bang on the corrugated iron fencing to encourage it to run fast. It was a cold and sometimes wet job. Later I graduated to judge's assistant and got to put up the scores on the judge's box. The most lucrative part of coursing for me was catching the dogs at the end of each race and returning them to the owners, many of whom were not fit enough to catch a dog. Sometimes an unscrupulous owner would give a dog a chemical 'sting' to increase its speed. In such cases the dog occasionally had heart failure at the end of the race and it was worth ten shillings ($1) not to bring it back near the stewards.

Len exercising Menang Chief

Uncle Joe always had greyhounds and I was engaged in walking them for exercise. His champion was called Menang Chief and won many important races.

Some years later we collectively bought Mum a small twin-tub Hoovermatic washing machine which she began to use. However, having always boiled the washing in a copper, she continued to do so after putting it through the washing machine first on the basis that it couldn't possibly be clean just by being machine washed. Mum invariably hung all the 'unmentionables' on the inside of the rotary clothes line and the sheets on the outside to screen the 'smalls' from view. Such was the modesty of the times.

Dad left the railways to work for the Shire Council as a labourer repairing roads or whatever other task was called for. For a time he operated the local swimming pool owned by the Shire. That pool was very popular and was the reason that we all learned to swim. We even had a water polo competition but without heating it was freezing on cold nights. Once the swimming club had an excursion to compete at Ouyen, 60 miles away. I hadn't entered for any events but wanted the trip. On discovering that we didn't have any entry for the tower diving I put my name down and got the trip. Competition day saw me walk three times to the end of the tower platform, with some trepidation, and plunge inelegantly off. No prize of course but the trip was good.

Len at age 14

After I had gone to Melbourne to work, Dad established a dry-cleaning shop in Hopetoun, the first ever. He was assisted by a cousin's husband who had experience in the business. Once when on holidays my wife Barb and I were to drive Dad's Ford Prefect utility from Hopetoun to Mildura to transport a baby that had been adopted within the family after her mother had died. To make the most of the journey in his car, Dad gave me the task of visiting each township between Hopetoun and Ouyen to establish dry cleaning agencies there.

At the age of 13 I joined the nascent cycling club organised, unsurprisingly, by Bill Kaye who owned a shop that sold electrical goods and bicycles. At first I rode my everyday Malvern Star bike manufactured in Melbourne by Bruce Small, later Lord Mayor of the Gold Coast. This was heavy and far from being a racing bike. I showed some promise on the track nevertheless and Dad bought me a Repco semi-racer, a compromise between an ordinary bike and a racing machine. After a couple of races on the track, road season began and the first race was a 10 mile event. Being young and new, the handicapper gave me five minutes start. I won by seven minutes and thereafter rode from scratch. The *Hopetoun Courier* sports headline that week read, 'Boy Makes Fool of Handicapper.' The *Courier's* cycling writer was cleverly called 'Spokesman'.

For the next few years I was heavily involved in cycling and raced in open company (all age groups) over much of north western Victoria with some success, even getting a write-up in Melbourne's *Sporting Globe*. My chances improved when we raced one day at the Hopetoun Agricultural and Pastoral Show. It was a track race handicap and each starter was given a push start by a helper. The pusher for the starter 15 yards ahead of me lost his hat as he launched his cyclist. He bent down on the track to retrieve it and I was off the seat, head down and winding up speed. I hit him amidships, went high in the air, my faithful Repco broke in two across both parts of the frame and I crashed heavily. Dad by this time was my greatest, perhaps only, fan and he straight away took the bike shop proprietor up to his shop and bought me a Max Rowley Special, a proper racing bike made by Hartley. I had that bike for the rest of my racing career and long after. Unfortunately, my cycling scrapbook got lost somewhere along the line.

Once on the track at Hopetoun I got sandwiched between two other riders and fell heavily, sliding a measured 20 yards on my back. My racing silks were ground into my back; no Lycra in those days. Dad held me under the tap near the football sheds, washed the debris away, and poured raw Iodine onto the abrasions. It really stung! However, I was back on the bike in time for the next race.

The Underbool Show, on the Mallee Highway between Ouyen and Pinaroo, once engaged our cycling club to stage events for its show day. The cycling track was ill-prepared and consisted of a narrow sandy strip around the football ground. It was overgrown with paddy melons (small wild melons) which burst as we rode over them and sprayed us with juice.

The goalposts had not been removed and one rider slid on the sand, caught his handlebars on the goalpost and did several very small circles of the post before disentangling. We eventually abandoned the bike races and I entered in the Underbool Gift (130 yards footrace). Having been in cycling training rather than running training and wearing cycling shoes, I needed an edge. When the starter called '*Get Set*' I started running and wasn't recalled for the break. However, I got caught just on the finishing line.

At the age of 14 I drove the old Chevrolet, now converted to a small truck, with all the cycling club members aboard, to various venues. After one of these excursions, the local policeman called round to see Dad saying, '*I know he can drive but keep him off the highway on Saturdays when there is football on.*' Commonsense policing!

I played cricket around the district with my father in one of the two Hopetoun sides and enjoyed it. I continued to play cricket in various teams over the years and today, at the age of 80, still keep wickets for my Rotary Club. I am also a life member of the International Fellowship of Cricketing Rotarians.

My sister, Janine, was born on Boxing Day, 8 days after my 14th birthday, in 1948 thus continuing the tight timeframe for family births, all four of us having been born within a three week period covering Christmas. I have speculated on this timing over the years and can only conclude that it is related to the onset of cold weather, no heating and no television. Janine was only two when I left home so our relationship has been long distance but a very good one over the years.

Local Culture

People from other ethnicities were quite rare in the area except for mostly second generation German farmers and another German, Peter Spiegel, who owned a garage. Hopetoun boasted one Italian (an eccentric grave-digger) and the Greek family of Theo Alfris who owned the Greek Cafe which was then almost obligatory in country towns throughout Australia. Curiously the cafe was named Bon Bon (French for 'good good'). It survives to this day and is a local institution whereas many others have come and gone. The only Aborigine in the town was a young lad named Elkin Reilly who had been adopted by the local doctor while he practised in Alice Springs. Elkin was a regular playmate for my brother Kel and me and later became a prominent AFL footballer for South Melbourne. That was about the limit of our exposure to other cultures. So too for foreign food. Garlic was unheard of and the only pasta was spaghetti and macaroni. There was no Asian food at all. Cheese was Kraft cheddar only and in blocks wrapped in silver paper. Table wine was unknown although shanty wine saloons in places such as the nearby village of Goyura sold 'fourpenny dark' port, the highly potent choice of alcoholics.

To be thought of as a local usually required a couple of generations of background in the area. Everyone was pretty much aware of everyone else's business and virtually everyone was known by a nickname rather than their given name. Nicknames were sometimes handed down from generation to generation.

Mutual help was freely given and because of remoteness it would have been difficult to function without it.

Political attitudes and voting were solidly Country Party in the federal electorate named Mallee.

Part Three
A Career is Launched

Finding a Job

In 1949 while still only 14, I finished Year 10 (Intermediate Certificate) and that was as far as the Hopetoun Higher Elementary school went. There was no money to send me away for further education so I had to go to work. My father, having been through the Great Depression, was anxious for all of us to have a government job because his idea of heaven was a guaranteed regular pay envelope. I had been awarded a Bursary to become a schoolteacher but that meant doing another year of education first. The local banks wanted to employ me, because of my school record, but again I had to do another year of school first. The Post Office took me in and thus began a public service career of more than 50 years. On my first day the Postmaster's wife, who lived in the residence adjoining the Post Office, took me aside and warned me off her six daughters in no uncertain terms.

I had the title of Junior Postal Officer and performed all the low level tasks in the Post Office. Delivering mail and parcels, delivering telegrams, sorting mail, cleaning and polishing brass plates and the counter surface, filling inkwells by mixing powder and water and cleaning the toilets. Every second week I would work night telephone exchange duty and operate the switchboard from 10pm to 8am. When things quietened down we were permitted to pull down the folding bed and sleep between calls. A four inch alarm bell was supposed to wake us. Sometimes I did both day and night duties. When I received my first uniform issue I felt that I really belonged. It was black double-seated trousers and a black tunic accompanied by removable embossed silver buttons. The buttons bore the Commonwealth crest and were accountable items, that is, I had to sign for them and return them when I left Hopetoun.

In those days pay came in cash in an envelope fortnightly. My first pay was four pounds four shillings and tenpence (about $8.50) and I tipped it out onto my bed and admired it. I had never seen so much cash. I still have my notice of appointment to the Public Service as a permanent officer at a salary of 170 pounds ($340) a year. I was a little upset to find that they deducted four shillings and sixpence (45 cents) a fortnight for superannuation. The Postmaster asked whether I wanted to elect to retire at age 60 or 65 because it affected the rate of superannuation contribution. At the age of 15 I couldn't even imagine ever being that old. I chose 65 on the basis that I would probably still be broke then; not too far from accurate! After retirement my hourly rate as a consultant was more than my original annual salary; of course it was 50 years later.

Once I had been sewing wheat bags during the day to earn extra money and was more tired than usual when starting the night shift. The wife of the local doctor was about to give birth and he wanted to call a doctor from a neighbouring town to attend but even the four inch alarm bell didn't wake me. Eventually he broke in through the window and woke me that way. When I had a medical examination for permanency soon after he said, 'At least I know that you sleep well'. He passed me as fit.

At the age of 15 I was quite naive. A 17 year old telephonist made a habit of staying after the end of her shift at 10pm and showing no sign of going home. I would pull down the bed to give her a hint to leave whereupon she would sit on it while I waited impatiently for her to go so that I could go to bed. It was some years before I realised what it was all about!

Notice of formal Public Service appointment April 1950

A literally shocking event occurred during a thunderstorm one night when shutters were dislodged by lightning strikes all over the area and kept setting off the alarm. It was necessary to plug into the line to check whether it really was a lightning induced false alarm or a live call. As I plugged in to one line to check, lightning struck it again and I found myself on the floor out of bed several metres away. Thanks to the lightning arresters, a pair of shellac coated carbon blocks fitted to the line with the other end earthed, no great damage was done.

One advantage of working the telephone exchange at night was that I was able to practice in the billiard room on my own during the day. The town billiard room was located behind the barbershop and opened officially only at night. However, the barber let me in to practise free of charge and I got a very solid grounding in skills that became useful later on.

Sometimes I rode my bike to the pictures (movies) at Warracknabeal 38 miles (61 kilometres) away and then home again afterwards. The movies were mainly black and white and featured Movietone newsreels that were full of interest. Training for bike racing was usually at 5am daily and involved a ride to Beulah, 16 miles each way. Riding the heavy Post Office bike with its load of mail during the day probably would have been enough training.

Another occasional extra job was delivering new tractors to farms for one pound a time. I drove them out, which took some time when they had no road gear, and then either rode my bike back or the garage proprietor picked me up.

The Big Smoke

The new Postmaster, Jim Dalliston, pushed me to think about a career and encouraged me to learn Morse code. He applied on my behalf for entry to the Postal Training School in Melbourne and claimed that I had attained a Morse speed of 12 words a minute. That was an extremely generous estimate but, being so remote from the District Office located in Ararat, no one came to test me and I was duly selected. Just after my sixteenth birthday I left for Melbourne to start the training. It was January 1951.

Uncle Joe came with me to help me find a place to live. After a week in Staffa House in Nicholson Street opposite the Exhibition Building, I settled in the industrial western suburb of Sunshine in a boarding house called Blair Atholl, named after a small town in the Grampians mountains of Perthshire, Scotland, where coincidentally my Ferguson ancestors had originated. It was directly opposite the Sunshine Harvester Works owned by H.V. Mackay and I was very familiar with the farm machinery they made. The boarding house was extremely rough and ready but it had the great virtue of being cheap. My salary was minimal even with a small living away from home allowance. After paying board of two pounds ten shillings ($5) a week and another ten shillings ($1) for a weekly train ticket to the city I had about one pound ($2) for everything else. At least the board included sandwiches, although barely edible, for lunch. Occasionally a letter from Mum and Dad would contain a pound note, which I knew they could ill afford, but it certainly helped.

Mrs Teese (known as Ma Teese) owned the boarding house and ruled it with an iron fist. I soon learned never to be first down for breakfast in the morning because the cat slept on the top plate in the pile of plates. The procedure was to grab a plate and line up. Mrs Teese deposited a handful (literally) of Weeties on the plate followed by a handful of sugar. She actually fried the eggs the previous night and warmed them up over water in the morning. I shared a small room with an elderly World War I veteran who was a kindly soul and had many tales such as his experiences as an Australian soldier in Cairo. Some of those stories were X-rated. The rooms had no door locks and it was a common occurrence for police to flash a torch on your face during the night. The establishment had seen several murders and some of the boarders were well known to the police. Ma Teese was a regular police informant.

A couple of Scotsmen shared one room, Sandy and Donald. Sandy was a former ship's engineer and Donald worked at the Werribee sewerage farm. Sandy was an alcoholic and from time to time went on extended benders. During one of these he drank a can of weedkiller belonging to Donald who insisted on charging him sixpence for it. No treatment was sought and the poison had no visible effect on Sandy.

I spent two years in that boarding house, being able to afford nothing better, before being called up for RAAF national service in 1953.

When I turned 18 I bought a second-hand 1952 Triumph Tiger motorcycle, 500cc twin cylinder with an *avant garde* sprung hub. This made it much easier to go home to Hopetoun for visits; previously I had travelled by train on the Mildura line getting on and off at the village of Lascelles in the middle of the night. For the next 60 or more years I continued to visit Hopetoun at every opportunity. However, I soon realised that going home meant slipping back into my local persona which I had no trouble doing. Despite my subsequent experiences and worldwide travel I never mentioned any of these things except in answer to a direct question. People whose whole lives were local would have regarded any such talk as boastful and intended to put them down. In later years I was invited on a couple of occasions to address the Rotary Club of Hopetoun on specific issues from my experience. The local newspaper, *The Hopetoun Courier*, also occasionally picked up something on my career or awards and ran it in a feature article along the lines of 'Hopetoun boy makes good'. My brother Kel, who became Chief Commissioner of Police in Victoria, made rather better copy for similar stories.

Triumph Motorbike and family outside home in Hopetoun 1953
L to R: Father George, mother Freda, Len holding Janine,
Rob and Kel.

The Chief Telegraph Office

The Postal Training School was situated at 126 Flinders Lane in the city of Melbourne. Each day we were trained mainly in Morse code and typing. Despite my lack of grounding in Morse code I picked it up quickly and had no trouble passing the progress tests. Touch typing was learned with covered keyboards making it impossible to see the keys. The typewriters were very old single case Imperials, Remingtons and Olivettis. My aim in going into the School was to qualify as a Postal Clerk and thus get back to the bush. I was unaware that the best Morse code students would be sent to the Chief Telegraph Office as telegraphists while the rest would become Postal Clerks. As a result, I graduated early and found myself working at the Chief Telegraph Office (CTO), 315 Post Office Place (Little Bourke Street), Melbourne.

Simple Morse key

Morse semi-automatic 'jigger' made by Melbourne Telegraphist Leopold Cohen

In those days telegrams were a major means of communication. Just after the war there was a two year wait to acquire a telephone and the majority of houses did not have telephones. The CTO employed about 600 people, mainly telegraphists. A network of telegraph lines radiated throughout Victoria and to some places beyond and telegraphists operated these lines in Morse code, sending and receiving telegrams. The other end of the lines terminated in Post Offices where Postal Clerks were the operators. A telegram originating at, say, Hopetoun and intended for, say, Portland would be transmitted to the CTO where it was received in Morse by a telegraphist listening to the dots and dashes in a sounder, translating those dots and dashes to letters, figures and symbols and typing them simultaneously onto a telegram form. (A dot or dash was determined by the length of time between clicks, a dash being three times longer time than a dot.) This was multi-tasking and skilled operators could listen, translate, type and conduct a conversation at the same time. The typed telegram was placed on a conveyor belt system that brought all the telegrams to a central circulation location where they were sorted and then distributed by hand to the appropriate outgoing line terminal, in this example, Portland. The telegraphist working the Portland line would then use the Portland call-sign to attract the attention of the Postal Clerk there and transmit the telegram. (Most lines served a number of Post Offices). At Portland it would be typed onto a telegram form and delivered by a messenger.

What now seems to be a quaint anachronism occurred at 10am each day, Australia being 10 hours ahead of Greenwich Mean Time (no daylight saving time then). Normal traffic was interrupted while a time signal was sent manually from the CTO on each Morse line. This comprised a series of dashes synchronised with the time signal that you hear on the radio. This allowed each Post Office to set its clock accurately each day.

High volume routes, such as Melbourne-Sydney, were served by Murray Multiplex (MUX) machines rather than Morse lines. MUX operated on 5-channel perforated paper tape. The five channels went across the tape in a line and the presence or absence of a circular perforation in each location determined the letter, number or symbol. (For example, the letter 'A' had a hole punched in positions one and two while positions three, four and five were not punched). The tape was prepared by a telegraphist typing on a keyboard that punched these holes in the tape, each message being prefixed by a channel code and the next number telegram in sequence. The tape was then run through a transmitter (by means of a ratchet engaging small perforations punched between positions two and three) over a landline and automatically converted to typing by a receiving machine at the other end where it would be torn off the continuous roll, checked and initialled. Any apparent errors were queried. Telegraphists could read these punched tapes as easily as reading a book. Sometimes errors could be corrected by cutting holes with a pocket knife to avoid repunching the entire message. Telegraphists would alternate between sending and receiving at the end of each hour.

In the mid 1950's these same machines were used to prepare input tapes for one of the earliest computers in Australia, SILLIAC, which was housed at Sydney University.

Very early in my life as a telegraphist I was warned by the Union for having too high an output per hour. I was told that this made it hard for others who were not so quick. Pride and stubbornness prevented me from slowing down.

There were some specialised Morse lines, for example, the line from the CTO to the Ford Motor Company in Geelong. A telegraphist was stationed at Ford and this line was used solely for ordering parts with telegrams addressed to the telegraphic code address 'Austraford Geelong'. These part numbers were complex being made up of letters and figures, from memory about 14 characters in length. Highly skilled telegraphists were necessary to get these part numbers right otherwise the wrong part would be supplied. Another dedicated line was to the Flemington Stock Yards for conveying market orders and prices between the stock and station agents and the growers. Still others were to the racecourses for conveying race results, newspaper reports and betting fluctuations. I worked at the various Melbourne racecourses almost every weekend for six years.

Once I drove my old (1947) Morris 8/40 Tourer car to work at Caulfield Races. It had a canvas roof and side curtains. Indicators had not yet been invented and hand signals were required to indicate an intention to turn or stop. To signal required pushing one's right hand out through the canvas flap in the side curtain. To avoid catching one's fingernails on the flap, it was necessary to make a bunched fist. As I neared the policeman on point duty I wished to indicate an intention to turn, bunched my fist and thrust it out through the flap with some velocity. Just at that moment a motorcyclist overtook me very close to the car and I punched him right on the point of the jaw. He wobbled dangerously onwards forcing the policeman to jump for his life. I believe that to this day the motorcyclist doesn't know what hit him!

We had a roster for what was called 'outdoor duties' and once I drew the Warrnambool Races, a three day affair. I went by train to Warrnambool, called at the Post Office to pick up gear, and got out to the racecourse. There I discovered that nothing was set up and all I had was a pair of bare telephone wires protruding from the wall. I had to install a relay, Morse key and sounder before I could start work. On that trip I learned a valuable lesson about gambling. The local Postal Clerk had two greyhounds entered in the speed coursing races on two nights of the long weekend. On the first night he told me to back the yellow dog, not the brindle one. The brindle duly won its race and the yellow was unplaced. The second night he reversed his advice and I backed the brindle dog. Yes, the yellow dog won. I learned that, if even the owner doesn't know, what hope does a punter have?

American made teletypes and British Creed teleprinters were used for some high volume telegraph traffic routes in the suburbs. We had pneumatic tubes running from the CTO to several newspaper offices around the City through telephone cable tunnels. Telegrams to and from those offices were fired in bulk through these tubes in carriers.

We also had the first transmission of newspaper pictures by wire. These were black and white and brought news pictures through in a matter of minutes. The pictures were wrapped round a revolving drum which was scrutinised by a light sensing mechanism then transmitted in binary fashion with the process being reversed to produce a picture at the receiving end. I particularly recall receiving pictures of the defector, Mrs Petrov, being rescued from her Soviet escorts at the Darwin Airport in 1954.

There were many humorous incidents at the CTO. One that appealed to me because it related to the small hamlet of Patchewollock near where I had grown up was an order for meat pies for their football pie night. The order was for something like ten dozen pies but it was mistakenly recorded as ten gross. The kangaroos must have had a feast as the train ran there only once a week. Another was a market order taken by telephone (phonogram) for six dozen fresh lettuce but the female phonogram operator heard 'French letters' instead. The Italian fruit and vegetable merchants at Victoria Market often sent telegrams about 'bins and pis'.

The CTO was staffed by many larger than life characters. One rode his horse to work in the centre of Melbourne, brought it up in the lift to the sixth floor then walked it up the stairs to the roof where he tethered it. He insisted that nothing in the public service regulations said that he could not; he was right about that although the regulations did allow for a forage allowance when your own horse was used on duty and another provided for a bicycle allowance for using your own bicycle. Another elderly man was a regular borrower of small amounts from his workmates. He scrupulously kept a list of people to repay but if anyone asked him for repayment he would ceremoniously transfer their name to the bottom of the list. This same man seemed to be addicted to tea as he sipped from an enamel mug all day. I eventually discovered that he kept his liquor in the adjacent large rubbish bin and refilled his mug from it quite frequently.

In those days smoking in the workplace was permitted and the main operating room, containing two hundred or so men at a time, was very smoky and there was no air conditioning. It was also extremely noisy with the sounds of Morse, typewriters, MUX punching machines, conveyor belts and the firing of pneumatic tubes, to say nothing of voices.

It became even noisier one day when, before the conveyor belts were switched on for the day, some of the larrikins placed metal ashtrays at intervals along every conveyor belt in the room. When all the belts were switched on the ashtrays progressed over the belt system and one at a time discharged into the metal collecting bin at the end. The effect was startling and had the Assistant Superintendent in charge in a frenzy. His name was Dick Boettcher and he was a fierce martinet, consequently the telegraphists used to do everything possible to upset him. He occupied a small office on the main floor but the partition did not go to the roof and was not secure. Each day the Assistant Superintendents would go through a pile of leave applications to approve them. One wag had climbed over the partition during the night, found an application for sick leave with the reason 'diarrhoea.' He rubbed some chocolate on the application and added the notation, 'sample herewith.' That caused another outburst from the volatile Assistant Superintendent.

Perhaps his most theatrical performance came when a mixed pair of mail sorters ventured up from the basement of the building to the roof and began very intimate proceedings unaware that they were up against the skylight of the main telegraph operating room. Cheers and whistles erupted and the whole room stopped work. The Assistant Superintendent charged out of his office to find out why, eventually located the cause and raced up onto the roof. So ended the entertainment for the day.

Many of the telegraphists had second jobs to make ends meet and one Joe Devlin was moonlighting as a shop assistant at the nearby hardware store, McEwans. He was a bit cheeky as it was only half a block from the CTO. One day Dick Boettcher came into the store. Thinking quickly, Joe came around the counter, picked up some merchandise, and said, 'Terrible rubbish they sell here isn't it Mr Boettcher.' He got away with it.

PART FOUR
TIME OUT FOR NATIONAL SERVICE

National Service Training

In 1953 I was called up for national service military training. Because of my telegraphy training, I was allocated to the RAAF in the 7th intake. This was for six months, the longest continuous training of the three services. I almost went to the Army because I did not act on the first couple of notices to attend for a medical examination. Reg Monkhouse, a Clerk in the Department of Labour and National Service who had been a Telegraphist, telephoned me via the lunch room at work to say, *'Listen you bastard. If you don't turn up for a medical on Wednesday you will be in the Army'.* I took the hint.

Beginning in March 1953, basic training was at No. 1 Stores Depot at Tottenham in Melbourne's west, close to where I was then living in Sunshine. There were three groups of trainees, each group called a 'Flight'. Mine was C Flight comprising 29 trainees and we were destined to become Telecommunications Operators. Flights A and B had to do with motor transport. Although it was still very warm, we were kitted out in heavy blue winter uniforms so that they would not have to issue both a summer and a winter uniform.

I was offered the opportunity to volunteer for active service in the Korean War and, thinking that it would be the only chance of my life to

Len in RAAF National Service 1953

travel overseas, I prevailed upon my parents to give permission. Luckily for me the Korean War was nearing a truce and no more national servicemen were sent. The ignorance of youth! My alternative explanation is that the North Koreans heard that I was coming and called it off.

An early lesson in military discipline and the powerlessness of lower ranks occurred when we were issued uniforms and rifles on the first day. The rifle was a Mark II Lee Enfield .303 calibre; a vintage weapon but nevertheless very effective. We were in ranks, handed the rifles straight from the armoury and then subjected to weapons inspection. I got two days kitchen duty for a dirty rifle that I had received only one minute earlier. The lesson was that military life is not going to be fair so do what you are told and don't complain.

We were housed in 16-bed huts, basic but weatherproof. The airmen's mess at Tottenham was being refurbished at the time and much of the cooking was done outdoors although we ate under cover. Days consisted mainly of military drill and trade training. There were plenty of chances for exercise, some compulsory. Occasionally we would draw sentry duty and patrol the base for a four hour stretch during the night. On one of these I encountered a man crossing through the stores compound and in my best military manner I jumped out in front of him with pointed bayonet (we had no ammunition for the rifle) and said, '*Halt! Who Goes There?*' in imitation of war movies I had seen. He nearly had a heart attack and turned out to be a cook taking a short cut between his house and the officers' mess.

A little excitement occurred one night when some of the trainees decided it would be good fun to turn a fire hose through a neighbouring hut. The water pressure overturned beds and sent everything flying. A brawl began between the occupants and their assailants and the duty sergeant turned up from the Sergeants' mess somewhat the worse for wear to restore order. It was like a Keystone Cops movie. Roger Cardwell, who became a prominent singer/entertainer, was one of the trainees and was most upset because his valuable guitar was hit by the water. He has never attended our reunions.

Another trainee was deposited, bed and all, in the middle of the parade ground while he remained asleep.

On Sundays we would march about three miles to Sunshine to attend church. The Protestants soon discovered that the Catholic Church meant a much shorter march overall and there were many conversions.

Small pox vaccinations were carefully calculated so that their effect would fall on our first period of weekend leave and most of the trainees were too sick to leave their beds. We were rarely given leave in that first three months so it rankled. Our medical orderly was a Corporal nicknamed 'Aspro Charlie' and that was about the extent of his medical ability.

Another incident occurred during bayonet training. Our Corporal instructor, Norm Jones (who was later murdered in Footscray while moonlighting as a taxi driver), put us through bayonet drill while himself armed with a long padded stick. Bayonet drill was largely by numbers finishing with a mock thrust through the body of the prone enemy. Norm didn't think that I was going hard enough and prodded me heavily in the face with the padded stick. Somewhat, well more than somewhat, nettled, I attacked him violently in the next set and finished by sticking the bayonet through his shoe and pinning him to the ground. He went deathly white and, on removing his shoe, found that the bayonet had gone between his big and next toe. He couldn't complain; he had told me to go harder!

To offset the lack of leave (I had a girlfriend at the time) I worked out a deal with one of the regular RAAF drill Corporals who was married and lived off base but had no transport. I had a motorbike but no leave pass. He gave me a regular airman's cap and jacket, I would drive off base with him as pillion, take him home and then go on to see my girlfriend. The regular cap and jacket got me back on base again without query by the guard at the gate. No motorbike helmets in those days. Regulars wore a peaked cap; trainees wore a Glengarry (the small cap worn on the side of the head and which had a very vulgar nickname based on female anatomy).

After three months of basic training, C Flight was transferred to RAAF Frognall, the communications headquarters. It was located in a beautiful old mansion on Mont Albert Road, Canterbury, in Melbourne's east. The mansion was the communications centre and four-bed huts and other amenities were arranged in the extensive grounds. The food was infinitely better than at Tottenham and four-bed huts were a real luxury. Leave was still scarce but we improvised as usual. Coir mats from the hut floors were thrown on top of the high barbed wire fence so that we could climb safely over. One of the group kept an Armstrong Siddeley car parked behind the base and I had my motorbike at the nearby home of fellow trainee Bruce Stevens' father who was the Mayor of Kew at the time.

Frognall Mansion
Radschool Association

We worked shifts in the Communications Centre which operated a torn tape system under JANAP (Joint Army Navy Airforce Procedure). Messages were on five channel tape which was manually transferred from point to point for onward transmission. The shift leader, Flight Sergeant Johannsen, liked to get me to send Morse to him for practice because it was no longer in day-to-day use in the Air Force.

One excursion by bus to RMIT in the city saw some of our number spend some time in a nearby pub. On return to base the Commanding Officer was waiting for us. The drinkers tried very hard to appear sober but the game was given away by a streak of vomit leading from one window of the bus.

In retrospect, military service was very good for me in those formative years. Discipline was useful and teamwork was essential. Friendships were formed such that after more than 60 years we still have an annual reunion and the bonds grow stronger every year. My friend Ron Hearn tells the story at every reunion of how I saved his life during a weekend, when the camp was otherwise deserted, by stuffing his mouth with mashed potato when he was bleeding to death after a tooth extraction.

I can well understand why some say that all young people should do National Service.

Resuming Civilian Life

Discharged from the RAAF, subject to three years in the Reserve, I went back to the CTO to work and to Sunshine to live. However, I found a new boarding house sharing a single room sleepout in North Sunshine with one of my friends from Blair Atholl. It was a little more expensive but my pay increased with each birthday although I was still on junior pay rates until I turned 21. The new place was not very salubrious and the landlady had a strange domestic arrangement whereby her husband slept in the garage while her boyfriend slept with her. Washing and ironing were supposed to be included in board but the service was so unreliable that I often had to buy a new shirt when going out. That gave me a large collection of white shirts.

I frequented a milk bar in Sunshine and became fond of lime spiders made with milk. I became friendly with a girl named Margaret who worked there. Another girl came to work there part-time and that was to have dramatic effect on my whole life. Her name was Barbara Stubbings and she became my wife for almost 52 years. Unbeknown to me at the time, Margaret warned Barbara off me but that served only as a challenge to her and we started going out together. She was 16 and I was not quite 19.

Barb and Len at debutante Ball 1954

Barb's mother had an objection to her pillion riding on my motorbike and insisted that I buy a sidecar for the bike; she regarded that as much safer. I duly bought a Goulding sidecar but as soon as we were out of sight Barb changed from the sidecar to the pillion. However, her mother rode happily in the sidecar and I sometimes took her into the city in it. One of my telegraphist mates, Neil Bloedorn, wanted to try out riding a bike with a sidecar so I changed places with him on one outing. We were crossing the Coal Creek Canal between Yarraville and Williamstown when the traffic tightened a little and Neil slowed down. Of course, when he did the sidecar momentum turned the bike to the right. Instead of compensating by turning the handles he slowed some more and the bike turned some more. In desperation he stood on the brake and the bike turned sharply right and flew off the parapet into the canal, narrowly missing oncoming traffic on the way. The tide was out and we landed in about six feet depth of oily sludge. The bike and sidecar had to be lifted out by a tow truck but neither of us was injured.

Neil found another way to injure me with the motorbike. I was adjusting the timing on the bike and found the timing cog a little difficult to settle back into place. I asked Neil to jiggle the kick-starter gently while I pushed the cog into place with my fingers. He gave it an almighty kick and I saw the severed end of my index finger going round and round in the now perfectly meshed cog. Much to my surprise it grew back after some months treatment with Ung Vita ointment, a fish oil based concoction.

Once I was ill and after three days Barb called round to see what had happened to me. She discovered that no one had attended to me

Resuming Civilian Life 71

Wedding day 1956

and told her mother who insisted that I move in to board with them. Barb later complained that she lost her piano because of that; it was removed to make room for her new bed. Barb's mother was a very feisty woman who ruled the family with a rod of iron. She did, however, have some inherent sympathy for underdogs and collected them around her. I suppose she saw me as one. Eventually she presented me with an ultimatum, 'Marry my daughter or find another boarding house'. With those options, what choice did I have? We became engaged in 1955 and married on 14 July (Bastille Day) 1956. She was 19 and I was 21. The wedding was in the Methodist Church in Sunshine and the reception in the Masonic Hall, Sunshine. The entertainment at the wedding was provided by Barb's cousin, Russell Stubbings, who was perhaps the leading tapdancer in Australia at that time and was frequently on television.

Our wedding night was at the famous Windsor Hotel in the city of Melbourne, by far the grandest place either of us had been in. It cost the enormous amount of 8 pounds ($16) for the night! Breakfast was silver service. Barb had been schooled by her mother to start from the outside and work inwards with cutlery so she did, but had a little difficulty with the size of the cereal spoon. When the waiter couldn't find the serving spoon for the bacon and eggs and brought another one we realised the error.

Next stop on the honeymoon was Mount Gambier en route to Adelaide. Approaching Adelaide in our old 1947 Morris 8/40 tourer car with canvas roof and side curtains we encountered a pea soup fog in the

Adelaide Hills and consequently were very late into the city. We were booked at the Park Hotel just out of the city area but on arrival there it was closed up and we couldn't rouse anybody. I walked up the fire stairs and through the hotel but still couldn't find anyone to let us in. So we headed into the city and chanced on the Grosvenor Hotel in the main street, King William Street. We of course had no booking and looked very young. In those days proof of marriage was just about necessary to get a room and they were reluctant. Barb's tears made them relent and we stayed there for a week, very obviously a topic of conversation among the staff. My first encounter with Adelaide water was running a bath. It filled with brown water and, thinking that something was wrong with the pipes, I let it out and ran another one. Repeating this process did not improve the colour and I eventually discovered that the water there, being drawn from the Murray River, always looked like that.

We drove towards my home town of Hopetoun via Renmark in the Riverland but in July 1956 there was a great flood. As we drove by Lake Barmera only the white line was visible on the highway. At Renmark the road bridge was underwater but we were able to lift the small car onto a railway flat car and cross the Murray River on the railway bridge. More drama on the road from Renmark to Mildura. For some inexplicable reason, Barb opened the door of the old Morris at about 80kmh. It opened from the front and thus caught the wind and, because she was holding the handle, it swung back and pulled her out of the car. Before she could fall I slammed on the brakes and the door shot forward again pushing her back into the seat. Almost a very short marriage.

In Hopetoun we tried the game of golf, the first time for both of us. Barb swung vigorously but mostly missed. The more she missed the more frustrated she became and the harder she swung. As a result, she hurt her back and the ministrations of the local doctor made it even worse. When we got back to Melbourne she could not stand straight and had to put up with many ribald comments associated with honeymoons.

We set up house in a flat attached to Barb's parents' house in Albion (West Sunshine). Barb worked in the city as a legal secretary for the firm Louis S. Lazarus and we both commuted to work by train.

I did apply for Officer Cadet training in the Army and was accepted but we would have been required to live apart for the first twelve months so I did not go on with it.

Now having responsibility as a married man, I began to think more about a career. Having reached 21, I was at last on an adult wage. After six years of service I had reached the minimum salary of a Clerk Class 1! I applied for and was selected to act as a Supervisor despite being considerably younger than almost all of the staff I supervised. At that stage the Commonwealth Public Service was arranged in divisions. Fourth Division contained those, like me, with a basic education. Third Division required the Leaving Certificate or its Public Service equivalent; Second Division was what is now the Senior Executive Service and First Division the Department Heads. It became apparent that my future depended upon further education so I sat for the Third Division examination and passed; that effectively allowed me to aspire to positions throughout the whole Public Service. I was prompted to sit for the examination by another telegraphist named Jack Nicol. He was an avowed Communist and very much 'agin the government.' We were not particular friends but he apparently saw something in me and insisted that I should take the examination, even handing me the application form; I owe him a lot.

I was eventually promoted to a supervisory position of Traffic Officer in the Chief Telegraph Office. I learned a good deal about supervision and management of people, some of it the hard way. After a while I was selected to go on the roster for the Test Room. That was the place where faults on the many telegraph lines were reported and it was our job to analyse the report, diagnose the problem then effect a 'fix'. Sometimes this required 'patching' lines around the State to circumvent a trouble spot. Patching was done by physically placing brass plugs into the spaces between brass blocks upon which were terminated the variously numbered lines. The instructions for patching were given to the relevant Post Office staff by Morse or telephone according to feasibility. It was necessary to know by heart the number of every operating and spare telegraph line in Victoria (and some beyond) and to know which Post Offices were on which lines. Having ascertained the approximate location of a faulty line section, we would arrange with the Engineering Division to despatch a line party to make the repair. The major interstate lines utilised carrier telephony deriving 18 or 24 channels over a single pair of telephone wires; quite clever technology for the times.

For a few years I taught technical telegraphy at night to telegraphists seeking to pass the salary barrier examination to allow them to progress to higher salary levels.

During the cricket test series Australia v West Indies in 1960/61 I was in charge of the Post Office at the Melbourne Cricket Ground which operated as a communication centre for the Press. I dealt with notables such as Sir Leonard Hutton, who had been knighted for services to cricket in 1956, and Australian cricket legend Keith Miller who were newspaper correspondents. A big plus was that I saw almost every ball bowled. I also discovered that some of the leading commentators had ghost writers and actually wrote little themselves. That test series was a remarkable one with the West Indies being captained by Frank Worrell and Australia by Richie Benaud. The West Indies team had some wonderful players such as Rohan Kanhai, Conrad Hunte, Gary Sobers, Wes Hall and Lance Gibbs. The Australian team included Bob Simpson, Colin McDonald, Norm O'Neill, Wally Grout and Alan Davidson. The series was closely contested and narrowly won by Australia 2-1. The West Indies team became immensely popular with Australian crowds and were given a parade in Melbourne in open-top cars to the cheering of enormous crowds.

I was not as lucky for the 1956 Olympic Games in Melbourne as I drew the equestrian events at the Oaklands Hunt Club. The Games were notable for the introduction of television in Melbourne. Sets were small, typically 17 inch screens, and in black and white. Somehow my mother-in-law procured one on time payment and evenings would see most of the inhabitants of her street sitting in pitch darkness watching this tiny flickering box.

In 1959 an automated tape switching system called TRESS was introduced so that messages received at the CTO did not need to be manually re-transmitted. This heavily eroded the need for skilled telegraphists using Morse. Moreover, the increased availability of telephones progressively reduced the demand for telegrams and the telegram service eventually disappeared in 1993.

Our first child, Ross Leonard, arrived on 10 August 1958 and the second, Travis Robert, twelve months and 13 days later on 23 August 1959. We learned two things from having two children so close together. First, that you definitely can get pregnant while breastfeeding. Second, never take a private room at the maternity hospital.

While Barb was pregnant with Ross, we made one of our many trips back to Hopetoun then went fishing on the Murray River near Ned's Corner Station with Dad and Mum. We arrived at the river in the late afternoon and hurried to erect a tent so that we could get in some fishing before dark. Evidently Dad and I in our haste cut too many corners and the tent blew down just after we got out of sight. We had taken an ice-cream shipper, a large canvas esky, in which to put the fish and we caught more than 200 fish that long weekend.

Most of the campsites on the Murray River were plagued by mosquitoes but Ned's Corner was relatively free of them. I recall another site at Nangiloc with Dad and Uncle Joe where we pulled in at night but didn't realise that we were under a peppercorn tree. The mosquitoes nearly carried us off. Nangiloc and Colignan were at opposite ends of a very long horseshoe bend in the Murray River. Astute observers will notice that each name is the other spelled backwards.

The growing family meant that acquiring a house was imperative. I worked up to four jobs at a time to save for the land and a house. One of the jobs was operating the newspaper kiosk Monday to Friday on the Yarraville Railway Station starting with the first train in the morning, about 5am, and finishing about 9am then going on to my normal job in the city. Shift work gave me some flexibility. On Friday and Saturday nights I worked as a night watchman at a local quarry from about 6pm to 4.30am. I also worked for the Electoral Office doing habitation reviews. Later I did some work for a newspaper office. I was charged, convicted and fined several times under the disciplinary provisions of the Public Service Act for engaging in outside employment.

During the late 50's I decided to take up athletics by running the mile race contested annually at the Telegraph Picnic. I trained quite hard and first competed in the event at the Whittlesea Showgrounds, north of Melbourne. The day turned out to be extremely hot, well over 100 degrees Fahrenheit. I went out quite quickly and on completion of the four laps required I was well clear of the field. However, instead of a finishing tape I was confronted with the Judge, Jack Boucher, telling me that I had another lap to run. I could not stop to argue so had to run another full lap in the searing heat. Some helpful soul threw a container of water in my face in an effort to cool me down but it was like hitting a brick wall. I managed to complete the lap and win the race and Jack, who by this time had been made aware of his error, was most apologetic. I could barely speak. However, someone had backed me and stolen the betting odds so all I got was eight pounds ($16) and a trophy.

The next year I contested the race again, from a scratch mark. It was at the Pakenham Racecourse south-east of Melbourne. On examining the track before the race I discovered that the grass had not been mown and was quite long so I decided to run in bare feet. This almost brought me undone because, just before the start, I found that someone had spilled a packet of drawing pins immediately in front of my starting position. On this occasion I narrowly failed to catch the outmarker and finished second. At that time the four minute mile had not yet been broken and I ran the mile in 4 minutes 30 seconds, bare feet and long grass notwithstanding.

I also began playing basketball, a sport from which I eventually retired at the age of 60. I played with Victorian Postal Institute teams in Melbourne. Early practice was in a church hall in the eastern suburbs. It was not ideal in that the ring at one end was above a stage and layups often meant falling up onto the stage. At the other end the ring was fixed to the end wall of the hall immediately above some stairs leading down to a sub-basement. Layups at that end often saw players crashing through the closed double doors and down the stairs.

Victorian Postal Institute basketball team.
(Len No.15)

I progressed through the grades and ended up playing several seasons of A Grade in the Business Houses competition at the new stadium at Albert Park where the main court floor was one used at the 1956 Olympics. Tuesday night training there was with Lindsay and Tony Gaze who became Australian legends of the game. When I moved to Canberra I immediately began to play with the Attorney-General's team in A Grade. By the time I retired all three of my sons were playing in the same team. As an illustration of the changes in average height over more than 40 years, when I began I was a tall centre player. By the time I finished I was a relatively small point guard. At the age of 60 my left knee needed arthroscopy and I decided not return after the operation. Barb said that I was too old in any case and, so that I wouldn't get fat and lazy, she enrolled me in a gymnasium, a practice that I have kept up for more than 20 years.

We bought a block of land in what was then Lower Plenty in 1959 for 475 pounds. While still paying the land off we managed to get a house built on 20 pounds deposit. It was a very small and basic weatherboard house with three bedrooms and was only eight and a half squares. It cost 3,500 pounds ($7000) and when we moved to Canberra we sold it for $13,500. The building company went broke before the house was finished and receivers came to finalise the financial arrangements. Fortunately for us, they knew little about the detail and we ended up without having to make additional payments. When Scott was born in 1967 we put a small extension on the house and installed a septic tank to replace the outside toilet. When the installers of the septic tank encountered rock I could not afford the fee for a compressor to get the rock removed and so I dug it out by hand with a crowbar. I was not very good with a crowbar so my father, who was almost 60 and by that time suffering what proved to be terminal myelofibrosis, kicked me out of the excavation and showed me how to dig.

Our boys went to Lower Plenty Primary School and I became Secretary of the School Committee (similar to a Parents and Citizens committee in NSW and the ACT). We were trying to get an oval built for the primary school but could not get any funding for it. I arranged for topsoil from building sites to be dumped behind the school and for the area to be levelled out to form a playing field. The Education Department approved the project but we did not anticipate that the soil would begin to move and encroach on the school building so the Department had to erect a fine retaining wall.

Our first house under construction

Family in 1969

Eventually the area became a small but excellent oval.

Another initiative was to sell shares to parents to build a cooperative library at the school. I think that this was the first such library in Victoria.

In 1961 I became a Freemason and have remained a member through the ensuing 55 years. I was Master of my Lodge in Melbourne in 1973/4 and First Principal of a Royal Arch Chapter in Canberra in 1983/4. I was made a Life Governor of the Freemasons Hospital in Melbourne in 1974 and am a Grand Chapter Officer having served on the active team in NSW and the ACT for a couple of years. Freemasonry is an old and not very well understood institution about which many myths abound. My view is that it is a force for good in the world and, while it may not make bad men good, it can make good men better. It is one of very few institutions that are open to men of all religious persuasions. It helped me personally in being able to speak in public and its rituals stimulate the memory. For the curious, Wikipedia provides a fair and balanced reference.

As Grand Director of Ceremonies, Masonic Royal Arch Chapter 1989

PART FIVE
CLIMBING THE CAREER LADDER

Traineeship

In 1962 I applied for a new three year training scheme called an Integrated Traineeship within the Postmaster-General's Department (PMG) at the equivalent of Clerk Class 4. This scheme aimed to turn out Traffic Officers Telecommunications, District Postal Managers and Mail Exchange supervisors all within the one training scheme. The first two years of training were common to all categories while the third and final year was devoted to the specific requirements of each group. An IQ test was a large part of the selection process and I was successful. The course also required undertaking a Diploma of Public Administration at the Royal Melbourne Institute of Technology (RMIT) but by part-time study in the evenings (for no extra pay). This Integrated Traineeship launched my Public Service career.

At that time the PMG was by far the largest employer of staff in the Commonwealth Public Service and was a huge organisation. We attended a series of central training courses on a variety of subjects and also gained on-the-job work experience in every Division and Branch of PMG. The major divisions were Engineering, Telecommunications and Postal but there were also large support operations like Personnel, Stores and Contracts and Accounts. We progressively sat examinations on a wide range of topics relating to our work experience.

Our Chief Instructor was Bert Groat who had previously been one of my instructors in the Postal Training School. Bert had a way with words and a very sharp wit. External lecturers came to deliver to us single lectures or a series and Bert thanked them appropriately after each session. We were highly amused on one occasion when he thanked a particularly tedious lecturer who had given a series of lectures by saying, *'The trainees are looking forward to your next lecture—which will be your last.'* It went right over the head of the lecturer.

For one section of the course a group of us spent a week at a regional office in Benalla. To save money, we decided to live in a camping ground and took our own camping equipment. Some of the wives came too. Lindsay Williams' wife, Lois, was in the camp during the day while we were at work when a snake wandered by. A passing man was prevailed upon to kill it with a shovel but he was obviously afraid and very tentative. He nevertheless hit the snake a couple of times. Lois decided to play a prank on Lindsay so she stretched the snake out half inside and half outside the tent. However, when she next looked the snake had contracted so she straightened it out again with her hands. This had to be done several times. That evening when she manoeuvred Lindsay to 'discover' the snake it had slithered away!

My third year of training was as a telecommunications specialist and involved every aspect of telephones, telegraph, data (or IT then in its infancy) and also their marketing and service. It even included an abbreviated telecom technician's course. The trainees really did integrate and the bonding was such that lifelong friendships formed and reunions are still held annually. The course was highly successful but it was so good that very few of the graduates remained in PMG for long. It had made them too attractive to poachers from other Commonwealth Departments. An ironic twist is that I was later given the task of evaluating the scheme and, as a result, it was shortened from three years to two.

Central Office, Postmaster-General's Department

At the end of the course I was allocated to Telecommunications Division Central Office in Melbourne in the Service Standards Section rather than to the Victorian State office. This was because of my consistently high marks over the duration of the course including those from RMIT.

After completing the four year Diploma at RMIT, I applied to enrol for part-time study in Commerce at the University of Melbourne. I had not reached matriculation level but the University accepted me on the basis of my RMIT results. This involved a further six years of part-time study which was completed in 1972. I finished with a double major in economics and a sub-major in business administration.

I was the first in my extended family to attend university and the first time I stepped on campus as a student I felt a sense of unreality about being there. They do say that the hardest thing about university is the enrolment procedure and that may well be right although finding the appropriate lecture theatre for the first time comes close.

Being a part-time student is a vastly different thing from being full-time. I found myself attending lectures at 7.15am, going into the city for a full day's work, then returning for lectures from 5.15pm eventually arriving home after 10pm. Money was not exactly plentiful so in the evening I usually went to the University Cafeteria, bought a bowl of plain boiled rice for 15 cents and added chilli sauce to it because that was free. This staved off the pangs of hunger until I got home. Another issue was that the full-time students commandeered all of the prescribed textbooks in the library and hid them out of their proper locations. As a part-timer it was rare to be able to find texts when I wanted them. I objected to paying compulsory student union fees when there was no practical benefit for a part-timer.

Once I was fogbound in Canberra Airport when an assignment was due back in Melbourne so I had to write it there. Upon submission it was marked A-minus with the comment that it would have been A-plus if I had listed the references I consulted. I thought it prudent not to mention that there were no reference books in the Canberra Airport.

In my second year at university my right hand stopped functioning for handwriting (Repetitive Strain Injury—RSI) and I had to switch to writing with my left hand. Having always had poor handwriting, I resolved that, in learning to write again, I would have copperplate writing. Unfortunately, the left handwriting looked very much like the right. As a group, telegraphists had been very closely studied for RSI which was then called Telegraphists' Cramp. A long study was done by a Professor Ferguson of the School of Tropical Medicine of all places. Sadly for me, RSI did not become recognised or compensable until many years later so I missed out. Changing hands did create difficulties with written examination papers because I could not fill as many exam books at first. Eventually writing became easier and I still write left-handed although I have recovered much of the use of my right hand and can write with it again, albeit a little awkwardly.

While at Telecom Central Office as a Traffic Officer Class 4 in 1966 I was given the task of reviewing the formulae (called coefficients) for staffing telephone exchanges nationally. Those coefficients had been virtually unchanged since 1915 and I challenged some of the basic assumptions upon which they relied. As PMG had about 45,000 telephonists at the time, the cost effects of errors in the formula could be significant. A significant flaw in the existing scheme, in my view, was to regard all of the time spent on each call as a single bloc when applying statistical theory to it. In practice, because of 'overlap' operating (working on two or more calls at once) the blocs should have been broken into segments and the calculation applied to those. My theory was accepted.

I established project teams in each State to conduct time measurements across the various classes of calls and types of telephone exchange. Some 85,000 observations were taken. The study had been designed with computer analysis in mind but, at that stage in the development of computers, programmers were a scarce resource. Being unable to procure a programmer, I attended a COBOL course for two weeks (COBOL not being the most appropriate language for mathematical work but being the only short course available). I then wrote statistical analysis computer programs that were not highly efficient but got the job done. A temporary setback occurred when the first program to run on our computers in Sydney was returned because it required a 16K compiler and they had nothing that big! Today 16K would be easily covered by a child's wrist watch.

Eventually the data were analysed, my report accepted and the findings implemented at a saving of 6.6% of staffing overall. This study gave me a reputation for handling major tasks.

While in the Service Standards area of Telecom a colleague and I were promoted in the same gazette. His name was Bruce Light. The promotion of Glare and Light in the one section caught the attention of the Melbourne Sun newspaper. If they had only known that one of our colleagues was Stan Moon they could have had Moon, Light and Glare.

I was sent to Bendigo in the Victorian Goldfields on an assignment and stayed at the historic Shamrock Hotel where I met the owner Joyce Evelyn Smith, the legendary 'Diamond Lil'. We played cards into the early hours of the morning. She was a fascinating character.

In 1967 I contracted Hepatitis A and spent five weeks in the infectious diseases hospital at Fairfield in Melbourne and three months off work. The

Director of Nursing at Fairfield at that time was the former Sister Vivienne Bullwinkel who was famous for being the sole survivor of the massacre of nurses by Japanese soldiers during World War II in shallow water off Radji Beach at Bangka Island in the Dutch East Indies (now Indonesia). As a curious coincidence we shared the same birthday. I am in fact writing this on the day she would have turned 100. By further coincidence, in 1977 she married Colonel Frank Statham who for a time headed the Commonwealth Department of Housing and Construction in Melbourne and with whom I had extensive dealings. She was a remarkable woman in many ways and was extremely kind to me during my hospitalisation. After convalescence I was fortunate in that the hepatitis left me with no enduring disability.

Sister Vivian Bullwinkel
Australian War Memorial Art 28389

To aid my convalescence, as I was very weak on release from hospital, my brother Kel took me fishing on the Gippsland Lakes. Fishing had always been a hobby for me and I thought that I knew a bit about it until I went to Cobram to collect the two older boys from a Scout Camp. They were going fishing with a lamb chop for bait. I told them that they wouldn't catch a Murray Cod with that bait but they brought back a rather nice one.

Our third son, Scott Kendall, was born on 4 June 1967. Barb had to cope with pregnancy during my absence in hospital. My father died in June 1968 at the age of 60 and was buried at Hopetoun. I had taken the baby Scott up to see him just before he died. Several months later I had the sad but happy task of giving my sister Janine away at her marriage to Graeme Poulton.

After the training course and transfer to Central Office, I had been promoted at Telecom within the same area, Service Standards, to Class 5 but in 1967 I applied for a Class 6 position in the Postal Planning area of PMG in Victoria and was successful. (I was simultaneously promoted as Chief Statistician in the Department of Civil Aviation but chose to stay with PMG). The work was entirely different being of a futuristic nature, looking into the future and coming up with new ideas. I did some work on an original idea of a computer controlled system for the collection of parcels and explored the use of cable tunnels for automated mail movement in the city area. However, after seven months an opportunity arose in the Central Office of PMG but this time in the Management Services area. I had come to the conclusion that the management field was where I wanted to concentrate because of its universality within the Public Service and that I needed to position myself with that in mind. I was promoted to Assistant Inspector Class 7 in the Organisation Section in 1968. I was soon promoted to Inspector Class 8 and then in 1970 to Senior Inspector Class 9.

During my period at Postal Planning I went one day in 1967 to the old GPO in Spencer Street, Melbourne, to meet with the Superintendent of Mails, Brian Moritz. While we were conversing in his office a fire broke out in the building. It started in an external mail elevator that carried mail from ground level to the top floor in bags. A welder was working there and sparks ignited the lint and paper at the bottom. The elevator shaft acted as a chimney and flaming bags of mail soon disgorged onto the conveyor belt system for distributing mail within the building. It was suddenly automatically distributing fire throughout the building. The conveyor belts themselves caught fire and the place became an inferno. My instinct was to flee but Brian started to go through the building to make sure that all his staff had escaped and I felt obliged to help him. We crawled over much of the building to keep below the acrid smoke but I was very relieved when Brian satisfied himself that no staff remained. We made it to the street, looked up, only to see a man leaping along the parapets on the roof. Apparently he was a lift mechanic who had been 'resting' up there and became trapped. Fortunately, the firemen got a long ladder past the tram wires and rescued him.

Our only daughter, Kylie Tricia, was born on 24 September 1969; we had wanted a daughter to complete our family and were very pleased to get one.

I need to record the enormous contribution that my wife Barbara made to my career. Putting her own study aspirations on hold, she bore the burden of being a stay-at-home mother while I acquired a tertiary education. She had always wanted to be a teacher but could not start her studies until I had finished mine and the children were all at school. Even then she got a job as a Special Teachers' Assistant at Cranleigh School for intellectually handicapped children in Canberra so that she would be home outside school hours. She did a teaching degree part-time but the authorities would not give her time off in her last year to complete the practical teaching segment because of her age. Once during my degree studies she took the children to my parents' home in Hopetoun so that I could do final study for examinations. The strange thing was that I found it difficult to study without them all around and even sitting on my knee while I studied so I asked her to come home again.

Barb had earned extra money while at home in many ways. She typed theses for university students, minded children, demonstrated craft materials, knitted fashion garments for advertising layouts and proof checked knitting patterns for Patons.

For some years I wrote courses and taught by correspondence students of Stotts College. The courses were mainly in public administration, management and related subjects. It gave me a small additional income as well as ensuring that I remained current in these subjects. While marking papers one thing that struck me strongly was that many of the students had very little idea of the use of punctuation. I was tempted to bundle up all the unnecessary commas and return them!

In 1971 area management was being developed for PMG Telecom and I was appointed Chairman of the Finance and Administration working party and also to the top level steering group for the project. My Working Party reported in 1972; most of its recommendations were adopted and subsequently formed the basis of Telecom/Telstra regional organisation when that was broken away from PMG.

Headhunted to Canberra

In early 1972 I was 'headhunted' by the Public Service Board in Canberra and the family decided to take the huge step of relocating. I had been assured of a career future in PMG but wanted to try my luck in the wider management field available in Canberra. I was promoted to Senior Inspector Class 11 (equivalent to the modern EL2) at the Public Service Board on 25 May 1972. As I was in my final year of a Commerce Degree at the University of Melbourne, I explored whether I could complete it at the Australian National University. That proved to be extraordinarily difficult. ANU, despite having started its life as a college of the University of Melbourne, did not want to grant me credit for all the units completed at Melbourne. The Public Service Board generously allowed me to operate out of its Melbourne office for the remainder of the year to complete my degree. We then moved to Canberra in December 1972, one week before the Whitlam Government came to power after 22 years in opposition.

Graduation from University of Melbourne 1973 with mother (left) and mother-in-law

At that time there was a strong move to centralise government departments in Canberra and incentives were offered for that purpose. Many houses were built by the government ('guvvies' in colloquial terms) and there was a waiting list to move into them. People were able to buy these homes from the Government at cost. As a desirable recruit I was given waiting list priority and allocated a basic four bedroom government house in MacGregor, a far western suburb of Canberra in the outer part of the Belconnen region and right on the edge of civilisation at that time.

The expectation was that we would rent for the three year current waiting period for government housing then be able to buy the house from the Government for its cost price of $12,600. On that understanding, we built a garage on the land. However, the Whitlam Government changed the rules without notice and without allowing current tenants to serve their time under the old rules. We either had to pay market price for the house ($28,000) or lose the garage we had built. We chose to buy and over the years extended the house four times. So much for a fair go from government!

Because of her experience of Housing Commission developments in Victoria, Barb was far from impressed with the house but soon set about making the most of it. We were among the first eight houses in the suburb and there were no facilities at all at first. Buses didn't service the suburb and the school had not yet been opened. Scott went to Latham Primary for the first year and the older boys went to Belconnen High. I was given observer status on the Latham Primary School Board for a year because MacGregor Primary was to open the following year, 1974. When it did open I was elected as inaugural Chairman of the School Board and continued in that capacity for some years.

I subsequently also became Chairman of the Parish Council of St Paul's Anglican Church at Kippax. For several years I was a member of Synod for the Anglican Diocese of Canberra Goulburn. I was Registrar of the West Canberra Australian Rules Football Club in the early days and my three sons played for the club. Scott, the youngest, had played 100 games before he was nine and went on to play senior football with the club.

Adjustment to Canberra was easy for me with work to occupy me but hard for the family. Barb had no extended family support and, in the early stages, very few friends to help out. The children had left all of their school friends and had to start again. In those days it was rare to find anyone who had been born in Canberra; practically everyone came from somewhere else so that the first question on meeting someone was, '*Where are you from?*' The social scene tended to be affected by public service rank and women were asked, '*What level is your husband?*' In some quarters it was almost a caste system emphasised greatly by some of the wives whose husbands were relatively senior.

I took up my work in the Organisation Division of the Public Service Board under the legendary Edward Stanley (Ted) Lightly who had been in Canberra since about 1932 and who knew everyone and everything. My work was essentially deciding what positions a department could have and assigning a classification (salary) level to them. With the creation of a new position went a funds certificate authorising the department to receive the money from Treasury to pay for it.

In those days classification was tightly controlled so that parity across departments would be preserved for work of equal value. In later years that control was dropped which led to great inequalities and injustices as well as allowing the better funded departments to outbid others for the best talent. Those bidding battles produced 'classification creep' which saw higher salaries being paid for the same work and today base level positions have almost disappeared. The Abbott and Turnbull Governments in 2015 seemed to be trying to restore some sanity to heavily top-ended organisations.

Another thing that has always troubled me is that in the public sector policy formulation is valued considerably higher than service delivery. This means that staff in direct contact with the public are almost invariably the lowest paid. I think that this is neither sensible nor fair. The primary business of public service is, perhaps tautologically, service to the public.

The new Whitlam Government came in with an agenda of making great changes in a short time and had accumulated a long list of things to do during its many years in the wilderness of opposition. It began immediately with a two-man Ministry being Prime Minister Whitlam and Deputy Prime Minister Lance Barnard. They held all the portfolios between them until other Ministers were sworn in.

I was given the task of creating a new Department of Northern Development and the Department of Tourism and Recreation, also new. Northern Development was under Rex Patterson as Minister. There had been an Office of Northern Development within the Prime Minister's Department from 1964 but the new Department was intended to reflect a fresh focus on northern Australia. Prior to the Whitlam Government the view had been taken that tourism and recreation were State matters rather than Federal and only three positions relating to tourism were available to be imported from Trade into the new Department. There was little guidance to be had on how these two departments should be structured or much detail about what they would do. It was largely left to my imagination in the first instance.

A third task given to me was to create a department, to quote the Prime Minister of the day, *'that even poor old Fred can handle,'* a reference to Fred Daly who was much revered within the Labor Party. This task resulted in the formation of the Department of Services and Property. It was something of a grab bag of different functions the largest being the provision of accommodation for Commonwealth activities.

My experiences were replicated pretty much across the public service at that time. There was little real planning, great haste and scant regard for the economics of changes. After the 1975 change of government the Whitlam

Treasurer, Frank Crean, told me that he would frequently explain to Cabinet that proposals brought to it were not able to be financed but they were approved anyway.

One of the more curious tasks I had at the Public Service Board came out of the Department of Services and Property which had responsibility for elections and referenda. It appears that Fred Daly developed a theory that the Labor Party would gain an edge in elections if it paid the Commonwealth Electoral Office staff higher salaries. I was tasked with undertaking a review of salary classifications as a result. This I did and concluded that a few positions should receive limited upgrades. Those findings were endorsed within the Public Service Board. I soon found myself called to the office of the Chairman of the Public Service Board, Alan (later Sir Alan) Cooley. Prime Minister Whitlam had complained to him that the upgrades were insufficient and should be reconsidered. Mr Cooley discussed the review with me and he then telephoned Whitlam to say that the review was a good job and fairly done and that he would not override its findings. He went on to say that if the Prime Minister wanted to upgrade the positions he would have to legislate for them. To everyone's amazement, Whitlam did legislate. The strategy clearly failed as Labor lost the next two elections. I was greatly impressed with the integrity of Alan Cooley as, to a public servant, a virtual demand from the Prime Minister is difficult to oppose.

One of the essential social skills at the Public Service Board was to be able to play cards, bridge and solo particularly. Lunchtime games (for money) were a daily occurrence and there were different grade levels. The top level bridge game included, as core members, Ted Lightly, Dave Gill and the Secretary of the Board, H B (Bruce) MacDonald. It was necessary to work your way up the ladder and be invited to join the premier school after relieving in casual vacancies over a period and proving your worthiness. I much enjoyed those games (and the modest profits).

I was allocated a portfolio of departments, most of which were based in Melbourne so that frequent visits to Melbourne were necessary. That suited me because of many family members in Melbourne.

One interesting task I had while at the Public Service Board was to create the first positions for Rangers at the Kakadu National Park in the Northern Territory. This was breaking new ground for the Commonwealth at the time.

Joining the Senior Executive Service

In early 1974 I applied for a Senior Executive Service Level 1 (now Band 1) position as Assistant Secretary, Operations, in the Attorney-General's Department. The most senior person on the interviewing committee was Deputy Secretary Ewart Smith who was a renowned expert in constitutional law. Ewart was a brilliant lawyer but knew and cared little about the management functions which the job I hoped to get entailed. He proceeded to ask a number of questions on constitutional law and was astonished (I think) that I could answer them because, by happy coincidence, I had obtained Honours in Jurisprudence and Constitutional Law at Melbourne University, the only law subject I took in my degree. I have always suspected that I got the job for the wrong reasons but in April 1974 I was promoted. This was my big career breakthrough, joining the senior executive ranks at the age of 39.

Assistant Secretary, Operations, covered in relation to the Attorney-General's Department proper, finance, internal audit, property & accommodation, lower courts of the ACT, management information & financial control and management advice for bodies within the Attorney-General's portfolio, policy oversight of the Commonwealth Reporting Service and policy formulation of fees and charges for courts. It also included security matters and advice to the Attorney-General on operational, administrative and financial matters relating to the Commonwealth Police and the NT and ACT police. Bodies within the portfolio at that time included the Australian Institute of Criminology, Australian Law Reform Commission, High Court of Australia, Federal Court of Australia, Family Court of Australia (from December 1975), Australian Legal Aid Office, Supreme Court of the ACT, Court of Petty Sessions NT, Industrial Relations Commission, Legislative Drafting Institute, Administrative Appeals Tribunal (from 1975) and Trade Practices Tribunal.

On my first day in the Attorney-General's Department I was sitting in a temporary office reading into my job when I heard a typewriter being operated with, to my practised ear, rare skill. I immediately said, '*I want that one as my Secretary*'. I investigated the source and met Charlotte McAuliffe who was also new to the Department. She became my executive assistant for the next 15 years, a very happy relationship. Charlotte was, and still is, something of a beauty and when Barb first met her she said, '*Don't tell me you picked her for her typing!*' I said, '*... well, as a matter of fact ....*' The two became great friends.

The Northern Territory engaged a good deal of my time in Operations. It did give me some interesting assignments such as visiting Ayers Rock by light plane with the Police Commissioner for the NT to negotiate the purchase of a former motel for a police station relating to the move of the old village at the Rock to Uluru. I also visited Aboriginal communities such as Yuendemu and Papunya to confer with the tribal councils. I negotiated with Peko Wallsend mines for accommodation near Tennant Creek in which to establish a police presence. If I recall the figures correctly, I obtained a police station and lock-up plus two residences for the princely sum of $20 a week. The police stations we were constructing around the Territory at the time cost almost $1m because all materials and labour had to be transported in. From Tennant Creek to Alice Springs the police had arranged for me to be transported by police car relay with a changeover at Barrow Creek.

During the break at the Barrow Creek pub I chatted with an American who was the publican's son-in-law. I noticed that the lintel around the open fireplace was missing and the American explained that, while drinking rum in the early hours of a cold morning, they ran out of firewood and fed the fireplace surround into the fire. Between Barrow Creek and Alice Springs we were travelling at about 150kph (there being no speed limit) on the Stuart Highway in the police car when a steer suddenly came out of the long grass onto the highway. We were closing very rapidly on its large rear end when, at the last minute, the steer veered left and we veered right.

Just before John Cain Junior became Premier of Victoria in 1982, he telephoned me about the old High Court premises at 450 Little Bourke Street Melbourne. This was the first home of the High Court in Australia and had operated in that Victorian State-owned building since 1928 under an arrangement whereby the Commonwealth had an option to purchase at a very low figure. The option had never been exercised and John Cain expressed his intention to terminate the option when he became Premier. As exercising the option would be a very good property deal for the Commonwealth, I approached Treasury for funds to exercise the option. To my astonishment, they at first refused. Eventually they relented and the Commonwealth completed the purchase. Some historic furniture from those old premises can be seen today in the High Court Building in Canberra.

Cyclone Tracy

On Christmas Eve 1974 Cyclone Tracy hit Darwin and devastated the city. The first report I saw on television on Christmas Day by great coincidence featured friends of mine, Keith Maynard (a fellow trainee in the PMG) and his family, who lived in Stuart Park. They were explaining that father, mother, four children and the dog got into the bath during the cyclone acting on the conventional wisdom that the bathroom was the strongest part of the house. There they stayed while everything above floor level was gradually blown away until only the water pipe tethered the bath. That too then broke and the bath, family and dog, were blown over the edge of the floorboards where they sheltered in the foundations of the house, amazingly uninjured.

Before the cyclone we had been endeavouring to get funding for the police boat based at Darwin because it was inherently unsuitable and it seemed that whenever it ventured to sea it had to be towed home by passing yachts. Try as we might we could not get financial approval. On Christmas Day the Police Commissioner, Bill McLaren, telephoned me with a situation report. I asked him, '*And how is the police boat Bill?*' He replied, '*It's OK*'. I said again, '*How is the police boat Bill?*' Again, '*OK.*' On the third time of asking he said, '*It's on the reef with its back broken.*' At last we got funding for a functional boat.

I was despatched to Darwin on Boxing Day to coordinate the Attorney-General's portfolio interests in restoring service after the cyclone. There was no accommodation to be had so I slept on the floor of the legal practitioners' robing room in the Supreme Court Building. It was one of the few buildings in Darwin that still had a roof. In deference to my rank, I was given a mattress on the concrete floor. The electricity ducts in the floors of the building were running streams of water. This I discovered by switching on a light in the toilet and a great sheet of flame leapt out.

Andy Hogg, the Department's administrative officer in Darwin, had encountered one of the hippie girls who previously camped on Lameroo Beach just below the courthouse wearing a Judge's scarlet and ermine robe inside the building. Somewhat scandalised, Andy said, *Take that off. It belongs to the Judge.*' She shrugged her shoulders and complied but proved to be wearing nothing else. I found a Judge's wig box but, on checking the contents, had to beat the seething mass of maggots inside with a stick.

A temporary canteen for the police and others of our staff had been established across from the Supreme Court in Mitchell Street using the skills of the lady who had owned the kiosk at Howard Springs, down the track from Darwin. That kiosk had been blown away. She was providing hearty meals and the police and staff were getting them free. After discussion with the Police Commissioner, it was decided to charge $1 a head for a three course meal. Not bad value.

The force of Cyclone Tracy was beyond imagination. Near the airport I saw the imprint of a refrigerator in a water tank some 80 feet above the ground. Huge brick columns supporting roofs were lifted upward and broken. Almost every part of the city was devastated.

I was told that the colourful Mayor, 'Tiger' Brennan, had been drinking rum on Christmas Eve to celebrate and knew nothing of the cyclone until he emerged on Christmas morning to find his city gone.

Police from every State and Territory had been brought in to assist and my neighbour from Canberra was one of them. I visited him on the wharf where he was guarding a large storage shed. I asked him what he was guarding and he took me in to have a look. It was filled to capacity with VB beer which had been imported for the Christmas rush. Greg said, *'In this climate they don't keep well and I have to condemn several each day.'*

During the emergency imported police commandeered vehicles and boats in rather cavalier fashion and I later had the task of negotiating with the owners about compensation. One brand new Mustang car had been taken over and the word 'Police' spray painted on its side. A sports-fishing boat had been taken over as a police boat.

Another amusing incident came out of the NT Police. A police officer, Peter Hamon, was in charge of a station down the track, Katherine perhaps, and wanted to repaint the premises. He pestered the Commissioner, Bill McLaren, about it and eventually offered to do the painting himself if the Commissioner would authorise purchase of the paint. Still he was refused. Shortly after Bill McLaren was on leave and towing his caravan down the track when it broke down nearby. Bill asked for help from the local police station. Peter came out to help and then booked the Commissioner for not having a current caravan registration sticker displayed. Bill McLaren copped it without complaint or retribution. Peter actually became the project officer for the new police boat.

On another trip to Darwin I was there over the weekend and drove down with the local Administrative Officer and one of his mates to the Mary River south of Darwin for a day's fishing. We were in a small aluminium dinghy on the river quietly fishing when we noticed a large crocodile quite close to us underneath an overhanging tree branch. On the branch was a sea eagle and only the eyes of the crocodile were visible. It waited very patiently for the bird to dip closer to the water. Eventually we decided to move the boat and when we started the motor the crocodile must have decided that it was now or never. It sprang vertically out of the water perhaps three or four metres and snapped at the sea eagle. It captured only feathers but the height of its leap was amazing. Unfortunately we caught no barramundi but plenty of catfish which the boat owner refused to let us keep on the grounds that they were inedible.

First Overseas Experience

Australia was to be host for the Sixth United Nations Congress on the Prevention of Crime and the Treatment of Offenders to be held in 1980 in Sydney Opera House. In 1975 I was appointed Deputy Australian Coordinator for the event, that duty added to my normal job. I had particular responsibility for the Congress administrative arrangements. I was sent to Ottawa to study the Canadian preparations for the previous Congress. I consulted Frank P Miller who had been the Coordinator for Canada and had a background in corrections. He was to prove most helpful and became a personal friend. This was my first official trip overseas and Barb came with me (at my expense of course). Frank died in February 2000 and I received a lovely letter from his wife Ruth letting me know.

I also went to UN Headquarters in New York to meet the chief of crime prevention and criminal justice, Gerhard Mueller. I was invited to lunch in the UN dining room and began to consider which of the fine international wines they would undoubtedly have would best go with my lunch. To my dismay Gerhard, thinking to make me feel at home, ordered Fosters Lager for me. Gerhard invited me to address a meeting of NGO's about the Sydney venue for the Congress. In 1975 I had never heard the acronym for Non-Government Organisations before but did not like to admit it and addressed them anyway.

Gerhard was married to Professor Freda Adler who was a criminologist and educator at Rutgers University. She and Gerhard invited Barb and me to their riverside apartment on the East River in Manhattan one evening. The view on the city side was directly to the Empire State Building but, on this occasion, the building was not illuminated. This did not deter Freda who simply telephoned the caretaker there, with whom she was on first name terms, and asked him to light up the building because she had visitors from Australia. A few seconds later the building lit up! We remained friends with the Muellers for many years and had the pleasure of hosting them to the opera at Sydney Opera House. I also met them again in Cairo.

The Congress was to be staged at the Sydney Opera House which led to detailed negotiations and inspections within the Opera House. That was very interesting and I learned such things as the details of helicoil springs that secured the seating and became familiar with the Green Room usually frequented by performers. As it turned out, the Congress was transferred late in the piece to Geneva because Prime Minister Malcolm Fraser refused to allow delegates from the Palestine Liberation Organisation (PLO) to enter Australia.

Before cancellation I was sent in 1978 to the League of Arab States in Cairo to publicise the Congress. The Head of the Department of Law in Western Australia, Roy Christie, accompanied me together with his wife Marie. We had the unusual experience of addressing a meeting of the Arab League of States about the Congress and answering questions. The proceedings were simultaneously interpreted in Arabic and English but at one point the electricity failed and the interpretation system ceased functioning. Undeterred, the delegates simply switched the entire proceedings to excellent English. I was impressed by the immaculate white robes of pure Irish linen worn by Arab delegates. The local custom of preceding every business discussion with hibiscus tea did not appeal to me much but it was a necessary protocol.

On the weekend the Australian Embassy staff hired a dhow for a cruise up and down the Nile and we joined them. There seemed to be plenty of Australian beer and wine supplied to facilitate trade missions. A very pleasant afternoon of sailing.

Roy and I were invited to a reception for Arab League delegates at the Police Academy on the River Nile island of Gezira within the district of Zamalek. We were delivered by the Australian Embassy Mercedes with driver and the approach to the Academy was a curving roadway flanked by Egyptians dressed in the manner of Bengal Lancers, each one holding a flaming torch. Spectacular! The receiving line of Police Generals on the red carpet led through an archway to a courtyard swimming pool. On the tiered seats on one side of the pool were the Egyptian members of a Scottish Pipe and Fife Band. The surface of the pool was covered with coloured balloons. A buffet or smorgasbord banquet was served adjacent to the pool. All of our care about what we ate in Egypt came to nought when we both suffered from the Pharaoh's revenge after the banquet because we had no idea what we were eating. I did recognise sheep's eyes staring at me from one dish.

We had arranged to go to the pyramids at Giza but Roy was too ill so Marie and I went. While climbing the close confines of the burial shaft to get to the main chamber of the Great Pyramid, Marie began to experience claustrophobia. At the bottom of a small staircase she found herself frozen and unable to go further. Our ancient snaggle-toothed Arab guide solved the problem by putting both hands on her backside and saying, '*Up Missy.*' I have never seen anyone go up stairs so quickly.

A trip to the Muhammad Ali mosque with Marie followed and a similarly elderly Arab guide must have learned his English from Australian soldiers. The mosque is largely built of alabaster and he held his torch behind the alabaster columns to show that we could see right through them. He accompanied this with a description for Marie's benefit, '*Look Missy. Bloody f**.cking alabaster, four feet thick.*' She didn't know whether to laugh or cry.

But I digress.

My first overseas trip in connection with the UN Congress on Crime was combined with another assignment. Because of my responsibility for oversight of the Commonwealth Reporting Service which provided transcript for Commonwealth Courts and Tribunals, I had been taking an interest in the development of computer assisted shorthand transcription. This emerged from the efforts of the CIA to use it for translating intercepted Soviet communications. The CIA did not have enough Russian linguists to cope with the amount of intercepted material and it was hoped that shorthand writers using stenotype machines could render the Russian they heard phonetically and that a computer could translate it into English. These stenotype writers would not necessarily know the Russian language. The idea did not prove practical but a derivative was that English speaking stenotype writers could render English phonetically and a computer could translate these stenotype outlines into transcript, initially with the help of a skilled note reader to make corrections and resolve homophones.

At the time the majority of shorthand writers employed by the Commonwealth Reporting Service used manual shorthand, mainly either Pitman or Dacomb. The shorthand writer recorded the proceedings then subsequently dictated the notes into a tape recorder for transcription by a typist. Usually transcription was only effected when a transcript was actually ordered. There was also the problem that the longer the delay between note taking and transcription the more difficult the process was. To produce a running transcript in major cases, that is, to have transcript available within a day, was labour intensive and highly expensive. There was also a shortage of skilled reporters.

After my UN Congress work had been completed in New York, I was joined by the Department's Director ADP (Automatic Data Processing, now IT) for three weeks to explore five systems under development. These were located in Chicago, Vienna Virginia, Los Angeles and two in the silicon valley of San Francisco.

In Chicago I visited the Stenograph Corporation which makes the shorthand machines and also was developing computer assisted transcription. The owner, Robert T Wright, invited Barb and me to his home in Lake Forest, a very nice suburb in the northern area of Chicago. He sent his chauffeur driven limousine to our hotel to pick us up. It was the first time that I had been offered drinks from a limousine bar. After taking us to dinner where we had Lake Superior whitefish tails, he was accompanying us back to our hotel when the discussion turned to the northern night sky. Next thing we were stopped on the side of the freeway admiring the northern lights (Aurora Borealis).

Stenotype machine.
Image–The Gallery of Shorthand

A humorous incident in occurred in San Francisco. My colleague said that he would like to visit the Museum of Erotic Art. Barb had previously observed to me that he seemed interested only in the seamier aspects of the cities we visited and she enthusiastically said that she would like to go too. I said, '*Are you sure?*' She said that it was the first cultural thing he had wanted to do. So we went. After a couple of minutes Barb was blushing more and more and soon rushed out of the building. She had thought that it was the Museum of Exotic Art! She then realised that she was standing under the sign outside so decided to hide in the bookshop until the rest of us got our money's worth (US$4). To make her presence in the bookshop appear normal, she bought a book entitled '*How Sex Can Keep You Slim*.' I have not a shred of evidence to prove that she ever read it.

The transcription systems being developed in the USA used a modified stenotype shorthand machine to produce a magnetic tape which could be fed into a computer to convert into transcript. Unfortunately, the process was not as simple as it sounds. The English language abounds with words and phrases that sound the same but have different meanings and are sometimes spelled differently. These ambiguities are compounded by the many instances where the first syllables of a word also form another word or words because there is no specific recording of the end of a word in machine shorthand. A human note reader uses context analysis to resolve these conflicts. While there were some simple context rules that computers used, this was the principal area of difficulty requiring human intervention at that time and editors who could read shorthand notes were used at first. The main rule then in use was to program computers on the longest match. Another issue is that shorthand writing is individualistic to some extent and there was a need for each writer to develop a personal dictionary to translate the shorthand outlines that they habitually used. For some tasks specific job dictionaries were also required to cope with words unique to that assignment, such as technical terms, names and places.

Despite the difficulties still being encountered at that time, I believed that there was great potential for one of these systems to be used in Australia by the Commonwealth Reporting Service and its State counterparts as well as by Hansard for recording Parliamentary proceedings. A report was produced in April 1976 and a further visit was undertaken in November/December 1976 in company with a new Director ADP, Terry Polleycutt, and a Court Reporter, Gary Elks, who physically tested some systems using his own machine shorthand skills. A new company had emerged in the intervening period between visits, namely Baron Data Systems based in

Oakland, California, and it had become the market leader. In short, approval was gained to purchase the Baron Data Systems product for $300,000 and it was able to be applied to any of the Australian systems. A favourable deal was obtained because of the marketing advantage to Baron Data in being able to claim international sales in the early stage of its development.

It was introduced immediately in the Commonwealth Reporting Service and proved successful. A showing to Hansard and State Reporting Service people was arranged in Melbourne in conjunction with a media launch by Attorney-General Peter Durack. A very skilled machine shorthand writer named Margaret Harnath was to do the demonstration. On the day before the launch I ran Margaret through the demonstration passage and it worked extremely well. I suggested to her that, because of the first law of demonstrations (akin to Murphy's Law), she might consider at the launch proper turning the magnetic tape over so that the computer actually transcribed the one she had done the day before which worked well. Came the day the demonstration went off without a hitch but afterwards Margaret told me that she was so confident that she had used the live tape. I would not have been so sanguine had I known that.

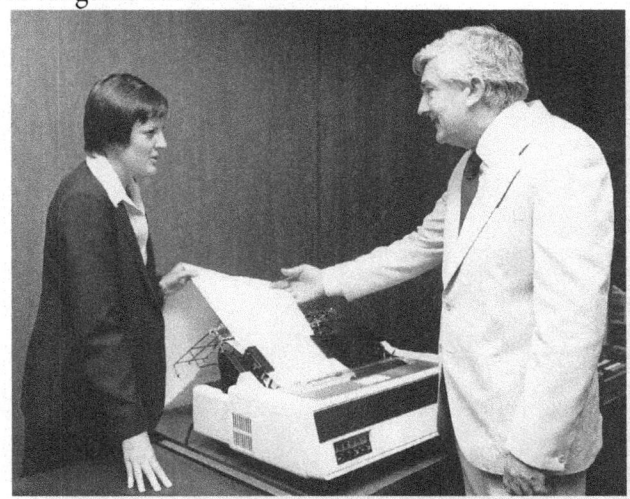

Attorney-General Peter Durack and Stenowriter Margaret Harnath at the Melbourne demonstration

The States and particularly Hansard did not immediately adopt the system because of entrenched resistance to change but now it is used universally. The logical development and improvements of this system are now visible as captions or sub-titles on virtually every television set.

Another Career Step

In 1977 the position of First Assistant Secretary (Division Head), Management and Special Services, became vacant when Kevin Crotty moved to become Clerk of the High Court and the Secretary, Clarrie Harders, decided to fill it on a temporary basis pending permanent filling which was going to take more than one month. He decided it on seniority and I was the junior of the two contending internal branch heads. Public Service Regulation 116 said that the criterion should be efficiency so I appealed, because to do otherwise would be to risk the temporary arrangement establishing a *status quo*. I was successful; I think the only appeal ever to succeed at that level. When the position was permanently filled I was again successful.

The Costigan Commission (officially titled the Royal Commission on the Activities of the Federated Ship Painters and Dockers Union) was held in the 1980s. Headed by Frank Costigan QC, the Commission was established to investigate criminal activities, including violence, associated with the Painters and Dockers Union. Its enquiries led away from union activities towards investigation of so-called 'bottom of the harbour' tax evasion schemes. This involved the asset-stripping of companies to avoid tax liabilities and was facilitated by criminals among the Painters and Dockers but benefited wealthy individuals (source: Wikipedia).

Costigan's report named three officers of the Deputy Crown Solicitor's Office in Perth, part of the Commonwealth Attorney-General's Department, as being complicit or derelict in their duties in relation to a range of 'bottom of the harbour' matters. One of these, a Senior Legal Officer named Abraham Bercove, was also accused of running a call girl service out of the Office. As statutory Chief Officer of the Attorney-General's Department, I was required in late 1982 to determine their guilt or innocence of charges laid under the Public Service Act 1922. I was able to determine quickly that Mr Bercove could not have been running a call girl service through the Office switchboard in Perth as alleged by Commissioner Costigan because the system at that time had no in-dialling. However, there was ample evidence to prove that he was involved in running a call-girl service and that he had been involved with his wife in performing secretarial services for a bottom of the harbour scheme. I found him guilty and recommended his dismissal. My decision was appealed as far as the High Court but was upheld. My chosen counsel in those proceedings was a promising young junior barrister from the Western Australian bar named Bob French who is now Chief Justice of the High Court of Australia.

Abraham Bercove had attended Perth Modern School and apparently had as classmates Bob Hawke (sometime Prime Minister), Alan Bartlett (became Deputy Chief Justice of the Family Court of Australia), John Stone (became Head of Treasury and a Senator) and Maxwell Newton (a prominent journalist). However, I had reason to doubt his legal skills when he put it to me that I was estopped from hearing his case. When I asked him what kind of estoppel he was arguing he looked at me in bemusement and asked, '*There are kinds?*'

I also found less serious offences proved against the other two lawyers charged and transferred the Deputy Crown Solicitor from his position in Perth to a non-managerial position in Canberra while a Principal Legal

Officer was reduced to Senior Legal Officer. After handing down these 'sentences' I first discovered what great lawyers some politicians were. They complained that the penalties were far too light without ever hearing any evidence in the cases at all. Only a great lawyer could judge that. It was a little strange for me, not being a lawyer, to have senior counsel appearing before me. One of them was Terry Franklin QC who showed me great courtesy; he later became a Supreme Court Judge in Western Australia.

The computer assisted transcription system that I had imported proved its worth during these hearings. I took Court Reporter Margaret Harnath, who had helped with CAT demonstrations in Melbourne, to Perth and she recorded 143 pages of excellent transcript in a single sitting day. At times I found it rather distracting to address conferences of court reporters, each of them recording verbatim every word I said.

Another interesting task came my way in 1985 after the fugitive Australian, Robert Trimbole, wanted on murder and drug charges, disappeared in Ireland in 1984 because there was no extradition treaty in place between Australia and Ireland under which he could be returned to Australia. I was asked to conduct an inquiry into why the treaty arrangements had not progressed between 1972 and 1985. I discovered that the first steps towards a treaty were taken in November 1967 when the Attorney-General's Department asked the Department of Foreign Affairs to approach several countries, including Ireland, about a treaty. A draft treaty was initialled in Ireland in 1970 but a need for legislative change and other minor points maintained a leisurely exchange of correspondence until 1977. The Irish, who were dragging the chain as much if not more than Australia, then confessed that their records were such that they no longer knew why certain wording had been agreed. A note on the Australian file a year later recorded an understanding that an Irish response was being awaited. Nothing much happened until January 1982 when the file was marked 'put away' by a person unknown. It was rescued by a new Branch Head at the end of that year as part of a review of extradition arrangements and in July 1983 work began on a draft model treaty. Discussions recommenced with Ireland but had not been completed by the time Mr Trimbole was arrested in Ireland in October 1984. A treaty was then put in place within days but, after an extensive legal battle, Trimbole was freed and disappeared.

Although it could not be proved from the files, it is my belief that work on the treaty was shelved because officers dealing with it in the Attorney-General's Department were planning a trip to Ireland to finalise the treaty when the then Secretary of the Department put it on his list as part of an overseas trip of his own. It seemed to me that the officers concerned then lost interest and did nothing to have it finalised by the Secretary.

One of my additional tasks was to serve on the Family Court Chief Judge's Policy Advisory Committee and one of my stranger jobs was to establish a *modus vivendi* between the inaugural Chief Justice (then called Chief Judge), Elizabeth Evatt, and her Principal Registrar, Ken Nixon. They were having some trouble establishing a good working relationship and the Chief Justice asked me if I could help. After separate discussions with them, I wrote a document proposing some rules of engagement for their professional interaction and they both accepted them. It seemed to work satisfactorily thereafter.

In 1983 I became Deputy Secretary of the Attorney-General's Department; the story of that appointment will emerge in a little more detail later.

I once applied for a course of study at the Administrative Staff College at Mt Eliza in the hope of brushing up some of my earlier management studies. The College was an adjunct of the University of Melbourne's business school. I was interviewed at the Public Service Board but refused enrolment on the grounds that '*You should be lecturing there, not attending the course.*' A compliment but not the result I wanted.

In 1983 a Judge of a Commonwealth Court had shown strong signs of becoming incompetent after many years on the Bench. In those days Judges were appointed for life and could only be removed by an address by both

Houses of Parliament in the one session, a course Ministers were reluctant to follow. I was sent to talk to him to endeavour to convince him to retire—a very delicate and possibly risky task. In the event he did agree to retire voluntarily. In 1989 when Secretary Pat Brazil gave me a reference, he spoke of me under the heading 'Sensitivities'. He wrote, '*One feature I end on. Len Glare has shown a capacity to deal deftly with sensitive areas. His role in helping to get the Family Court under way, for example, showed that he had the ability to deal with complex and sensitive matters. I can give more recent examples, particularly in interpersonal problem areas.*' I think that the retirement episode was probably one of those in his mind.

Senior Executive Fellowship

In 1988 I was awarded a Senior Executive Fellowship to study human resource management around the world for three months. Barb accompanied me. During this time, among other things, I worked with ICI in London, visited the London School of Economics, delivered a lecture on change management to INSEAD (the International School for Advanced Management Studies) at Fontainbleu in France, visited Stuttgart University in Germany, consulted a management academic in Zurich and worked with Fujitsu in Japan. On arrival in Japan I received a letter from Fujitsu saying, 'Dear Mr Grare. We hope you had a present fright.' I hadn't expected that the spoken peculiarities would come through in the written word as well. Similarly, on a weekend trip to Lake Hakone near Mount Fuji I got a restaurant bill that included 'One Grass Whine.' I still have it; the bill not the wine.

At INSEAD I arranged to meet a professor for discussions over breakfast at my Fontainbleu hotel before he flew to England. He asked me to order his breakfast, boiled eggs. I agreed but after hanging up the telephone struggled to recall how you said that in French. None of the staff at the hotel spoke English. Eventually I got it, '*Les oeufs a la coque*'. Why they use that term I still do not know.

In Stuttgart Barb became ill with a urinary tract infection and I went to a night chemist to try to get some medicine. I was very nearly arrested while trying to mime a urinary tract infection. My German language skills were slender indeed. Having procured the medicine, I then had to wait until the night porter came on at the hotel (he spoke English) to find out whether you were meant to drink this medicine or if there was an alternative more fundamental use.

The lady in charge of the dining room at the Stuttgart hotel spoke no English and I spoke no German so we communicated in imperfect French. At the end of dinner I wanted to ask for the bill and asked for '*le billet* (the ticket)' instead of '*l'addition* (the bill)'. She brought me a beer ('bière').

In Zurich we had booked no accommodation so went to the tourist advisory desk at the station. I must have been looking particularly poor that day and we were sent to the Franz Josef hospice run by nuns. It was a little austere and breakfast comprised bread rolls with no butter (in the European fashion). At least we were allowed to share a bed. Next day we moved.

In the U.S.A. I was put on their overseas visitor program which included working with Bank America, Levi Strauss and General Foods. I also visited a farm in Minnesota owned by a State legislator and several establishments in Connecticut. I went to Washington DC and consulted a number of Congressional committees and also to Cornell University in New York State. In Newhaven, Connecticut, we stayed in the Melba Inn which, like many things in Newhaven, was named for the Australian soprano, Dame Nellie Melba, who performed there in 1894. The US Overseas Visitor Program assigned me a local volunteer driver to get me to appointments and generally show me around. Her name was Marion Stone and she was zany but delightful. I began to have doubts about her driving when she drove up the down ramp onto a freeway. She later met us in New York for dinner but her car was broken into while we dined and her overcoat stolen. One of my meetings in Connecticut was at the home of a Bank America senior executive who had a beautiful wooded property through which deer roamed freely.

We stopped briefly in Denver, Colorado, to attend a technology conference and found that the Chief Justice of the Family Court of Australia, Alastair Nicholson, and his Principal Registrar, Bill Johnston (now Justice Johnston) were also attending and we joined forces. Alastair and I had served together on the Council of the Australian Institute of Judicial Administration and Bill and I had worked together in the Attorney-General's Department. We spent a day on the weekend doing a tour by SUV of the high country, elevation in excess of 10,000 feet. We drove on the 'Oh My God Trail' and were told that it got its name from the time when President Theodore Roosevelt was driven over it in a horse-drawn vehicle by a driver who didn't like Roosevelt's politics. The driver whipped the horses furiously around hairpin bends on precipitous slopes causing to Roosevelt to repeatedly exclaim, 'Oh My God.' I could well understand why. For dinner we went to a Wild West themed restaurant in Denver called 'The Buckhorn Exchange.' Waitresses wore buckskin and animal trophy heads adorned the walls. On the menu were Rocky Mountain oysters and Barb, having not had oysters for several months, ordered them without pausing to wonder where in the Rocky Mountains you would get oysters. They came out piled high and coated with breadcrumbs. After a little exploration she pronounced them rather chewy. We then told her that they were bullocks' testicles. After gagging for a while, she donated the remainder to the rest of us.

Denver is a mile above sea level and on the steps of the Capitol Building (State Parliament) there is an inscription marking that altitude. It is said that in Denver you can join the mile high club without having to pay an airfare.

On return to Canberra I discovered that the Department had a budget crisis essentially because some senior lawyers did not understand the difference between commitment and expenditure and had over-committed the Department by some $3m. It was too close to the end of the financial year to get back on budget track. Despite not even being in the country or my own job at the time, there was some attempt to make me the scapegoat. This persisted even after I left the Department as was reported to me by a

Judge when two senior Departmental officers attended a Court Conference at Twin Waters in Queensland. I suggested an action for defamation might ensue and did not hear that allegation again.

Probably as a result of my fellowship, I was asked by a Parliamentary Committee to present to it the case against performance pay in the public sector. John Taylor, the Auditor-General of the day, presented the case for. As a result of my studies around the world, I had concluded that performance pay in the public sector did not work well. Its usefulness in the private sector seemed to depend heavily on secrecy about amounts actually paid to individuals. The real difference was often slight but recipients usually did not know that. In the public sector there is more transparency so the bluff factor was less likely to work. The US Navy had tried a performance pay experiment at its China Lake facility and that was unsuccessful. A further problem in the public sector is that amounts set aside for performance bonuses are likely to remain static year by year or even be reduced in real terms because of arbitrary budget decisions, so-called efficiency dividends and inflation. Recipients would have an expectation that their bonuses would increase year to year but certainly not reduce and public sector budgets made that inherently unlikely. The motivation studies of Herzberg had shown that a satisfied need is not a motivator but an unsatisfied need is a demotivator. Also, in the public sector, performance feedback is often a charade of 'going through the motions.' Honesty in the feedback is secondary to getting the process ticked off as finished. My own experience, even when performance pay was not involved, highlighted this when one of the boxes to be ticked was 'Where could the candidate improve performance?' The Secretary of the Department could not think of anything to improve and asked me to provide something he could write down. Naturally I invented a 'motherhood' statement that did me no harm but satisfied the interrogatory.

In the event I won the performance pay debate and the Parliamentary Committee recommended against it. However, the Government of the day introduced it anyway and the outcome seems to have been as I predicted.

Unfair differences in executive remuneration between Departments have resulted because some have more budget room than others. It seems that all of this has belatedly dawned on Government after many years.

The years 1983 to 1989 were probably the peak of my public service career in many ways. Having reached Deputy Secretary level in the Attorney-General's Department without being a qualified lawyer, I had wide ranging responsibilities including the national management of legal aid and bankruptcy. I was a Member of the Department's Board of Management, (an initiative of mine and the first such Board in the Commonwealth public service). My portfolio included corporate services, information technology, finance, human resources, public relations, court reporting service, corporate and strategic planning, buildings and property including courts, Ministerial and Cabinet liaison, resource planning, parliamentary committees, technological change, industrial relations and security.

Additional appointments held included:
- Chairman, National Advisory Committee on Computers and the Law
- Member of the Council of the Australian Institute of Judicial Administration
- Director and Chairman of Law Courts Ltd
- Senior Executive Responsible for Equal Employment Opportunity
- Member of Family Court Chief Justice's Policy Committee
- Member and Secretary's Deputy on Industrial Democracy Committee
- Chairman, National Human Resource Planning and Development Committee
- Chairman, Resource Coordination Committee
- Chairman, Program Budgeting Steering Committee
- Chairman of two Acquisition Councils (major purchases exceeding $6m)
- Chairman, ADP Major Projects Steering Committee
- Member, Information Technology Committee

During this period I was made a Fellow of the Australian Institute of Management.

The range of experiences coming from the additional appointments listed above as well as the broad scope of my primary responsibilities potentially opened a wide range of career opportunities for me, considerably broadened my outlook and experience and introduced me to many contacts for networking.

My standing had come to the point where, when the job of Director-General of ASIO became vacant, the *Canberra Times* named me as a leading candidate calling me 'effectively the administrative head of the Attorney-General's Department'. Deputy Secretary Frank Mahony of the Attorney-General's Department, who had acted for a period as Director-General of ASIO, counselled me strongly not to consider the job. That advice became academic as I did not get the offer.

All of this came to an end in March 1989 when Pat Brazil retired as Secretary and his replacement, Alan Rose, redefined my job to make it able to be held only by those with formal legal qualifications. Essentially, this meant that I was out of job and on track to be declared redundant at the age of 54. Before dropping this bombshell, Alan Rose delegated to me the task of telling nine senior executives, including a couple of division heads, that they were no longer required. It was a task that I did not enjoy, especially as I thought his judgment was wrong in relation to most of them. When that was done it became my turn. I still recall the shock of being told the news and I responded defiantly that I was not finished yet. That proved to be true although at the time I had no idea how I could make it happen. The then Solicitor-General of the Commonwealth, Dr Gavan Griffith, came into my office on hearing the news and asked rhetorically, 'Are they barking mad?'

In his book '*Not An Ordinary Life*', David Evans, at that time head of the Protective Services Coordination Centre, wrote of this period, 'There must have been a 'Night of the Long Knives' in AG's because my friend Len Glare, the Deputy Secretary of the Department, had been given an office in another building, away from the seat of power, no doubt to force his resignation through perceived loss of status.'

My demise was probably ensured when I gave a farewell speech at a function for a couple of the senior executives made redundant in which I observed that the Attorney-General's Department must have been in great shape to be able to afford to lose officers of that calibre.

While my potential redundancy process was going on, I arranged with the Chief Justice of the Family Court of Australia, Alastair Nicholson, to do some work for him as advisor on a major review of the Court's administration being undertaken under the chairmanship of Justice Neil Buckley. I also reviewed security in the Court which had become a major issue.

The Family Court of Australia became administratively self-governing from 1 January 1990 and Chief Justice Nicholson appointed me to act as Chief Executive Officer from that date, pending permanent filling. Before taking up the position, I had a short holiday on the south coast of New South Wales but on 28 December 1989 Newcastle was hit by an earthquake. I left the beach and travelled to Newcastle, although not formally being CEO, to see what I could do to help with the Court's facilities there and to show support for the local staff. I believe that CEO's have a responsibility to do that even if there is nothing practical to be done at the time.

On 1 January 1990 I took up the position formally but the Court's principal office was then in Sydney so I commuted from Canberra Monday to Friday each week. This was intended to be for a short time but it ultimately took eight years to get the head office to Canberra. For that period I usually caught the 6.30am flight out of Canberra on Monday mornings and the 6.40pm flight home on Friday nights (voluntarily flying economy class). This imposed a great strain on Barb, having to run the family and household on her own but she never complained. My main problem was eating out every night by necessity and longing for a home cooked meal on return. However, Barb had the opposite problem and wanted to eat out on Friday nights. Needless to say, I took her out!

On the issue of where the central office of the Court should be located, in a special issue of the Court's magazine on 26 March 2004 to mark his retirement as Chief Justice, Alastair Nicholson, wrote:

> 'When I came here the Court was very Sydney orientated and at one time I wanted to bring the offices to Melbourne. That was resisted by the CEO (me) and staff, which was correct because it would have perpetuated the same problem. I think the move of the National Support Office to Canberra was a very good one—this really is a national organisation and the national office should be in Canberra.'

PART SIX

ATTORNEYS-GENERAL AND OTHER INTERESTING CHARACTERS

Attorneys-General and Spy Flights Over Tasmania

My career has been enriched, or at the very least made more interesting, by the characters I met and some I worked with.

My second day in the Attorney-General's Department in 1974 found the Secretary of the Department, Clarrie (later Sir Clarence) Harders taking me over to Parliament House to meet the Attorney-General, Lionel Murphy. Clarrie told Lionel that I was to be in charge of the latter's pet project of establishing a network of legal aid offices around the country. It emerged that six were to open in six States over the next fortnight with a great blaze of media activity. However, apart from premises we had practically nothing ready. That was the first time I had heard of it. With a great deal of effort from many people we managed to get them open. I was perpetually afraid that someone would look at the law books on the bookshelf behind the Attorney-General during the television interviews and discover that they were only dust jackets.

Lionel Murphy had a vision of legal aid offices being places where a shirt-sleeved lawyer would sit in an open space among the poor and needy clients dispensing legal advice that they would never be able to afford in the private system. I am not sure whether he got this idea from American movies but, in practice, neither the lawyers nor their clients wanted to work quite like that. The lawyers wanted conventional offices and their clients wanted privacy.

The Australian Legal Aid Office persisted for a number of years until the function was eventually largely returned to the States and Territories. The Attorney-General, Lionel Bowen, and I did a tour of Australian capitals in a Government VIP plane to sell the States on the idea of taking it back. I had the unusual experience of being the only passenger in a VIP aircraft when I boarded in Canberra and we picked up the Attorney-General in Sydney. He sent me alone to Darwin because he regarded that as a lost cause but, surprisingly, I secured their agreement. At that time much of the funding for legal aid came from interest earned on solicitors' trust accounts and interest rates were running as high as eighteen percent. This 'guaranteed' the States and Territories a sizeable amount of money and, astonishingly, none of them seemed to consider that these historically high interest rates might not last. When rates inevitably fell they found themselves having to supplement the funding with large amounts of their own funds. I thought I deserved a medal for making that deal for the Commonwealth!

In early 1975 I was in Canberra Hospital after a minor operation when Lionel Murphy pulled me out and sent me to Hobart with the then Commissioner of Commonwealth Police, Jack Davis, to negotiate a deal with Tasmania in relation to their police training facility. I dragged myself out of the hospital and onto a plane to Hobart. On arrival there we found that, because the Tasman Bridge had fallen, we had to undergo a long detour to get to the city and therefore arrived at our hotel about 10pm. At reception the metal shutters were being erected for the night and, while I was registering, the heavy steel end post for the shutters fell and hit me on the head. I was knocked to the floor and could hear the Commissioner, Jack Davis, yelling *'sue the bastards!'* Not feeling very well to begin with, I asked whether the bar was open so that I could restore myself a little. It wasn't but they offered to sell us miniature bottles of whisky. Jack and I ordered one each but when delivered they turned out to be 500ml bottles. We nevertheless drank them and I felt much less pain.

Next day we met the Tasmanian Labor Attorney-General, Bill Neilson (later Premier) to discuss the police training facility. My instructions from Lionel Murphy were vague in the extreme and I sought some enlightenment from Mr Neilson. He said the purpose of the meeting was to get some Commonwealth money into the facility. Nothing came of the exercise. On my way home the Fokker plane went Melbourne-Albury-Canberra but at Albury they tried to offload me. I was feeling rather ill and weak but managed a strong performance with the airline and retained my seat.

I was later sent on a similar mission to endeavour to acquire the Trades Hall Council building in Davey Street, Hobart, to convert to Commonwealth Law Courts. This was prompted by a factional fight within the ALP about building new Trades Hall Council premises in the suburbs but that could not work without selling the Davey Street premises. Fortunately, on this occasion it was a very good location for Commonwealth Courts despite the factional motivation and the deal was duly done. Design of the new building had to retain the Georgian streetscape and the building was constructed within its Georgian facade. This was the first time I had seen a computerised simulation of a proposed streetscape.

Lionel Murphy was the first of ten Attorneys-General with whom I was to work over the years. Most of them were interesting and Lionel was perhaps the most interesting of all. He was a strange mixture of idealism and lascivity. He was a strong proponent of legal aid and the reform of family law, particularly to remove the doctrine of fault from the latter. He also had Ministerial responsibility for film censorship and wanted me to provide a 16mm projector at his home so that he could view contentious movies there. However, he had a reputation for inviting young women to view doubtful films with him so I resisted. Eventually he let it go. He also established the Civil Marriage Celebrants program as an alternative to religious ceremonies. By some strange coincidence, most of his early celebrant appointments were comely young women whom he had met socially.

Lionel had a connection with Ethiopian Airlines, I think through his wife Ingrid. This led him to meet Junie Morosi who had an airline background and who was to become well known in political circles. In May 1974 Al Grassby lost his Parliamentary seat in the Riverina and was subsequently appointed as Commissioner for Community Relations within the Attorney-General's portfolio. He established a temporary office in the Administrative Building which housed the Attorney-General's Department. Lionel Murphy arranged for Junie Morosi to work as an assistant to Al Grassby and Lionel became a frequent caller to the office on evenings when only Junie was there. A member of my staff reported sensitive observations about these meetings. However, Junie also met other Ministers and was offered a job as Principal Private Secretary by the Treasurer, Jim Cairns. A public scandal ensued and eventually Jim Cairns retired from Parliament in 1977. In 2002 Cairns confirmed that his relationship with Ms Morosi had been sexual.

In February 1975, just after the Terrigal Conference of the ALP, Lionel Murphy was appointed to the High Court of Australia on the recommendation of Prime Minister Whitlam. Lionel always claimed that he had no inkling that he was to be appointed and offered as evidence that fact that Neil Sainsbury, formerly of the Attorney-General's Department, had been transferred to the High Court as project officer for the new building. He said that he would never have countenanced the transfer if he knew that he was to go there himself.

Lionel subsequently became embroiled in legal proceedings concerning a solicitor named Morgan Ryan (who Lionel had famously called his little mate) that required his frequent attendance in Sydney. In respect of these visits his staff lodged movement requisitions to the effect that he had been engaged on High Court business. However, he did not sign these personally as having undertaken the travel for High Court purposes and I declined to pay him travelling allowance until he did. After about three months he eventually signed them.

After these few encounters I thought that Lionel would not be favourably disposed towards me but I nevertheless applied for the position of Clerk (CEO) of the High Court in 1983. In due course I was summoned to be interviewed by all seven of the High Court Justices together. As the interview proceeded, I found that Lionel was becoming more and more of an advocate for me almost to the point of embarrassment. When it began to appear likely that they would offer me the job, I explained that I also had some expectation of being offered a job as Deputy Secretary of the Attorney-General's Department and that, if I had the choice, I would accept that job. The remainder of the interview consisted of asking me which of the other candidates I would recommend. I did get the job as Deputy Secretary. This experience heightened my long held view that Lionel Murphy was an extremely complicated person but he clearly was not one to hold a grudge.

Keppel Earl (Kep) Enderby, a former Canberra lawyer, succeeded Lionel Murphy as Attorney-General in February 1975. He was reported as having once solemnly assured Parliament that *'most of our imports come from overseas'*. The Department's media officer, John Dickie, told the story of a time when there was a security scare and a police guard post was placed outside the Enderby residence. One night the Enderby family cat came down the driveway, stepped onto the roadway, and was skittled by a car. The young police officer on duty observed it gasping its last in the gutter and, as an act of mercy, reversed his revolver giving the cat several blows on the head with the butt. He then took the cat up to the house and explained to Mrs Enderby that the cat had been run over. Several nights later Kep appeared at the guard post asking for the young constable who had been on duty that night. On being told that he was not on duty, Kep said that he just wanted to thank him and asked that the others tell him that the cat was doing fine but that the Vet said that concussion was still a problem.

Kep directed that <u>all</u> correspondence for his signature was to conclude with the words, 'With best wishes, yours sincerely, Kep Enderby.' This led to the rather odd result that his letters to Commonwealth prisoners who had sought his intervention to gain parole would sometimes contain words to the effect that, 'You are the greatest bastard in the world and I am going to leave you in gaol until you rot. With best wishes, yours sincerely, Kep Enderby.'

Parole applications once took an odd turn when the Senior Legal Officer who handled them and who kept a very untidy office, stacked a number of parole files on top of his wastepaper basket overnight. Inevitably, the cleaner took them and they went to the rubbish tip.

Once I was travelling with Kep by air towards Brisbane and we were flying over the Gold Coast looking down on all of the mansions built on canals when Kep mused, *'We need to start a legal aid office down there. There are a lot of needy people.'*

It was during the Enderby era that I first gained particular insight about political advisers in Ministerial offices. He had three of them at one stage and I went with Secretary Clarrie Harders, a vastly experienced senior public servant, to the Attorney-General's office where Clarrie attempted to give Kep sound and impartial advice. Kep turned to his 'three stooges' and asked, *'What do you think?'* The three answered to the effect, *'We think whatever you think boss.'* Kep turned to Clarrie and said, *'You see!'*

Kep lost his job as Attorney-General when the Whitlam Government was sacked by Governor-General Kerr on 11 November 1975. I recall that the staff in his office became quite hysterical that day. He subsequently became a Judge of the Supreme Court of NSW and I encountered him in the basement car park of the Sydney Law Courts Building in Queens Square. He smiled and came towards me as if to greet me and then suddenly stopped and said, *'I am sorry. I thought I knew you.'*

When the news of the Whitlam sacking came through, I was at lunch at the Italian Club where I had been arguing that the Governor-General would have to sack the Government because it seemed to be trying to act illegally to raise funds to pay public service salaries. In fact, I had thought that the sacking would have happened before the previous public service payday. To me it was a question of illegality and the Government's inability to provide for a functioning public administration, not one of politics. The sacking nevertheless became hugely controversial and split the community, creating probably the most dramatic political event in Australian history. It has remained a *cause célèbre* for Labor supporters ever since. An amusing small incident occurred when Whitlam returned to Parliament House from Government House and encountered Paul Keating going down the front steps. Keating had only very recently been appointed to the Ministry. As they crossed paths Whitlam said to Keating, '*You're sacked!*' and kept walking. Keating was astonished wondering what on earth he had done.

The Australian people rejected the Whitlam Government at the ensuing election and Malcolm Fraser, who had been appointed caretaker Prime Minister by Governor-General John Kerr, became Prime Minister.

Ivor Greenwood became Attorney-General for a few weeks when the Fraser Government came to power and then Bob Ellicott was appointed. Bob had been Solicitor-General for the Commonwealth before entering Parliament and was therefore well known within the Attorney-General's Department. In the lead up to the 1977 election, Bob went to Tasmania and the electorate of Bass, then held by the Liberal Kevin Newman, was a well known marginal seat. Bob sought a briefing before going to Tasmania and I strongly advised him not to agree to a new Family Court Registry being created in Launceston (within the Bass electorate) because it was not justified by the amount of business there. He listened carefully and assured me that he would not succumb to blandishments. Before he returned to Canberra I read a media announcement that a new Registry would be created in Launceston. When he returned I asked him what happened. He gave me a whimsical smile and said, '*I couldn't resist their arguments*'.

Peter Durack replaced Ellicott as Attorney-General in September 1977 and held that office until the Coalition lost government in March

1983. He was from the well-known Western Australian pioneering family and was a delight to work with. Barb and I were invited to his suite at Old Parliament House for Christmas drinks. Barb was chatting with him and said, '*I know your face but I can't recall your name.*' He replied, '*Oh, my name is Peter*' and continued chatting. He was very unassuming and my career didn't suffer at all from the gaffe.

When Justice Sir Ronald Wilson was appointed to the High Court his swearing in was held in Brisbane where the High Court was on circuit at the time. I was to attend and to take along his Commission from the Governor-General that he would receive during the ceremony. On receiving it the night before going to Brisbane I discovered that it had not been dated. I telephoned the Governor-General's office and was asked to write the date on it. I had known Justice Wilson in his former capacity as Solicitor-General for the State of Western Australia so it was not entirely inappropriate. Early in his life Ron Wilson had been a railway clerk and had learned to type. Even as a Justice on the High Court he kept an ancient typewriter in his office and typed much of his own correspondence.

I remember that swearing in for another reason. Peter Durack was to attend and speak in his capacity as Attorney-General and John Dickie, the media adviser, took him into a small room opening off the main corridor to robe. Peter was having great difficulty getting into his formal legal attire and John was attempting to fix his tie and vest. In the process, Peter's trousers were dropped around his ankles out of the way. Just then the door to the corridor was opened and the assembled dignitaries got a good view of the Attorney-General of the Commonwealth standing there with his trousers down.

In March 1983 the Hawke Government won power and Gareth Evans became Attorney-General. Previously a law lecturer at the University of Melbourne, Gareth had been highly critical of the Attorney-General's Department while in opposition. He had announced his intention to cut a swathe through it when he became Attorney-General. I had the task of preparing the brief for the incoming Attorney-General in the event of a change of Government. I researched all his public utterances and found some 93 topics affecting the Department. I organised and compiled a brief on each of these topics and on the Sunday morning after the Saturday election this brief was handed to him. He was astonished that the Department he had so heavily criticised for inefficiency could produce this material but he still felt that he had to deliver on his promise to make changes at the top. Alan Neaves was the incumbent Departmental Secretary at the time and he was appointed to the Federal Court of Australia as a Judge and was replaced by Pat Brazil a week after the election. I remember Alan asking me, perhaps rhetorically, whether he should accept the offer of judicial appointment. As he would be entitled to Commonwealth Superannuation and also receive his judicial salary and eventually a judicial pension as well, I think he must have been joking.

Alan Neaves had come from being Commonwealth Crown Solicitor to be Secretary in 1979 and had not had much to do with administration before that. I had a very cordial relationship with Sir Nigel Bowen, Chief Justice of the Federal Court of Australia, and Alan asked me to come with him for a courtesy introductory visit to Sir Nigel in Sydney when he first became Secretary. Sir Nigel had an excellent grapevine network in Sydney and, whenever I was there, he would discover it and I would get a message to call on him. He would tell me about problems in the Court and current prominent cases and which Judge he had assigned and why. He would explain the legal nuances of various cases and I gained a very good informal legal education from him. Before we went into Sir Nigel's chambers I explained to Alan that we would know how we went with Sir Nigel if, at the end of discussions, he offered us a drink. If it was a beer we would not have done very well. If it was a whisky, not so bad. If it was a single malt we would have done very well. At the end of discussions and right on cue Sir Nigel offered us a single malt.

At one stage Sir Nigel was interested in combining all of the federal courts into one administrative unit and asked me whether I would accept the role of CEO. His vision did not come to fruition during his tenure because of judicial sensitivities but more recently something similar has happened. A much earlier proposal by Sir Garfield Barwick was a system of Judicial Administration covering all of the Commonwealth Courts under which he would effectively be the Chairman of the Board.

The new Secretary of the Department, Pat Brazil, responding to pressure to improve the management performance of the Department, promoted me to Deputy Secretary in April 1983, the only non-lawyer ever to reach that level in the Department. This brought me into frequent close contact with Gareth Evans only one month into his ministerial career.

Gareth was a very interesting character. Possessing great intellect and a self-admitted large ego, he was a challenge for those who worked with him. He had a caustic sense of humour and was quite at home with self-mockery. For example, he told us that his colleagues at the University of Melbourne had given him a large empty box as a farewell gift to carry his ego to Canberra. He had a fiery temper and was known to throw files at his staff from time to time. He also had an enormous capacity to absorb a brief on one reading and little patience with those who tried to tell him anything twice. It took us a while to get accustomed to his methods. Correspondence to him was, as is the general practice with Ministers, sent on to the Department for the preparation of a suggested reply for his signature together with instructions as to how to treat some of these representations. One Ministerial endorsement had us puzzled; it read 'T E F E'. The combined might of the senior officers in the Department couldn't decode this so we asked to be enlightened. The response was that it meant 'Tell 'em f**k 'em'.

He was also a devotee of the *Yes Minister* TV program and one letter came to us with the Ministerial instructions consisting of a series of drawings of small round objects. It emerged that this was taken from the *Yes Minister* program that had Minister Jim Hacker, too polite to write 'balls', endorsing it 'Round Objects' to which Sir Humphrey responded *'Who is this Round and to what does he object?'*

One day Gareth was to speak at the Hilton Hotel in Sydney and he was subject to credible threats of assassination at the time. I accompanied him to the Attorney-General's suite in the Sydney Law Courts building and arranged for him to be fitted out in a Kevlar vest. We then walked side by side down to the Hilton Hotel. On the way, it suddenly dawned on me that Gareth and I were a similar height and build and we both had beards. I began to hope that the gunman knew what Gareth looked like!

Gareth once read in the newspapers an opinion piece contradicting his own views by my brother Kel before his appointment as Chief Commissioner of Police in Victoria. Gareth expressed some astonishment saying that this was not what Kel had written for him in a University assignment. I replied, *'Gareth, he had to pass your course.'*

Gareth was well acquainted with the famous Geoffrey Robertson QC and I was once given the task of negotiating with Geoffrey to do a *Hypothetical* TV program to publicise legal aid.

Perhaps my most notable experience with Gareth arose from the Franklin Dam case in the High Court. The new Hawke Labor Government had enacted legislation and regulations to prevent clearing and excavation of the Franklin River Dam site. The Tasmanian Government ignored both. The Commonwealth approached the High Court to prevent the State of Tasmania from constructing the Franklin River Dam on the grounds of environmental damage to a wilderness area of national importance containing significant Aboriginal artefacts. Indications were that construction was continuing in spite of the application. Attempts to obtain evidence on the ground in the wilderness area were thwarted by threats of violence to the Federal Police. Having some knowledge of the capabilities of the RAAF with high altitude infra-red photography, I suggested that the RAAF might be approached in the first instance to see whether they had routine training flights over the area that might produce evidence as to whether work was continuing. This suggestion was approved by Gareth Evans but enquiry revealed that they did not have such routine material. However, the RAAF suggested that it could be done as a special flight if properly authorised. There was discussion about that proposition and Gareth asked me whether he should consult the Defence Minister Gordon Scholes. I replied very strongly in the affirmative. The Defence Minister agreed to the flight and I was given the task of coordinating this with the RAAF.

Pat Brazil, Department Secretary, congratulated me on a 'brilliant' idea. I responded, rather prophetically as it turned out, that it would be alright if nothing went wrong.

Eventually it was arranged that an F-111 would fly over the area and take photographs on a given day. The aircraft would fly at a high altitude and would not be readily visible or audible from the ground. The internal signal that went to Fighter Command at Glenbrook in the Blue Mountains said, 'Aircraft to attract as little attention as possible.'

On the morning of the scheduled flight the RAAF told me that they had been unsure whether the F-111 would be serviceable that day so had put a Mirage fighter over the area to take photographs the previous day. The Mirage flew at an altitude of about 300 feet and made several passes up and down the valley at about the speed of sound. That certainly did attract attention but about all the blurry images showed were bulldozer drivers trying to crawl under their machines. In the event the F-111 did fly on the appointed day and took beautifully clear pictures, one of which was subsequently signed by the High Court Justices who sat on the case and is displayed in the ANU staff law library. With this evidence, the Commonwealth won its case in a judgment handed down in July 1983 and so the Franklin River was 'saved'.

The Mirage flight of course attracted the attention of the media and the saga became 'Spy Flights Over Tasmania.' Gareth became caricaturised as *Biggles* and a great political brouhaha erupted. All of this was featured in an ABC TV *Four Corners* program about Gareth's transition to a Ministerial role. I appeared on the program and the ABC kindly sent me a copy of the tape. On the tape is a sequence where Gareth, while guest speaker at the National Press Club, offered what he termed 'the streaker's defence'. *'It seemed, Your Worship, like a good idea at the time.'*

Many attempts to play this up politically in Parliament ensued but it eventually all petered out with Gareth and me both intact in our jobs. Despite the execution of the idea going wrong, Gareth did not hold it against me. In fact, when he left the Ministry he asked me to see if I could place his Melbourne-based Commonwealth car driver, Dominic, with Alastair Nicholson, the Chief Justice of the Family Court. This was duly arranged.

Lionel Bowen succeeded Gareth as Attorney-General from December 1984 to April 1990, Gareth having become Minister for Foreign Affairs. Lionel was also Deputy Prime Minister and strongly influential within Government. He was very much Sydney oriented and had little interest in Melbourne so when I was trying to secure a site for the Commonwealth Law Courts Building in Melbourne he showed no great enthusiasm. Eventually he agreed to come to Melbourne and look at possible sites. As an inspired thought, I took him to Jimmy Watson's in Carlton for lunch and he was much taken with it. Afterwards he looked at the Flagstaff Site on the corner of William and Latrobe Streets, opposite the Flagstaff Gardens and above the Flagstaff underground railway station and endorsed its acquisition. It proved to be an excellent choice.

The Commonwealth Courts building program is a story in itself. The Department had been trying for a long time to establish an orderly program for constructing Commonwealth Law Courts buildings in each of the capital cities. Cabinet put us off on the first occasion by asking for further development of the proposal. Eventually a more highly developed proposal was put to Cabinet but on the day it was to be considered Lionel Bowen was overseas and the Justice Minister, Michael Tate, had the task of arguing the case in Cabinet. Michael was junior and not a member of Cabinet and was quite nervous. In Cabinet the proposal was met with negativity and Michael did not offer much resistance. I was forced to assume argument of the case and was fully expecting to be thrown out when Paul Keating, then Treasurer, who had said nothing up to this time, suddenly offered a smaller amount of money over ten years. I countered asking for a much larger amount over five years, still expecting to be thrown out. Paul Keating responded with an amount in between the two over seven years and I said 'done'. Thus was the program established. To this day I don't know what motivated Keating and can only assume that he thought it was a good proposal.

Lionel Bowen had Ministerial responsibility for Film Censorship and it was his task to make appointments to the Film Censorship Board. The usual practice had been to recommend to the Attorney-General appointments made on the basis of experience in arts, literature or films. However, every such recommendation we put to him was not approved. Acting on the basis of something I heard him say about wanting to bring average suburban values to the Board, I put forward a recommendation for appointment of his 'average western suburbs housewife mother of four' and it was approved. It wasn't the worst appointment ever made to the Board either.

Some Attorneys-General had no great appetite for film classification and I was sent to Sydney to view and report on contentious films from time to time. One was *La Grande Bouffe*, a 1973 film where four Frenchmen tried to eat themselves to death over a long weekend. I didn't feel like lunch after that one. *Caligula* was another film I had to view.

A long-standing veteran of the Film Censorship office was Lin Kirkwood who had seen it all, literally, over many years. One day he uttered a dry pronouncement in a very bored voice and I have never forgotten it. He said, *'There is a fortune waiting for anyone who invents another human orifice.'*

Lionel Bowen was a very good Attorney-General to work with having a great deal of commonsense as well as useful influence within the Government. Towards the end of his tenure I moved from the Department to become CEO of the Family Court of Australia. When the new Family Court of Australia was opened in Goulburn Street, Sydney, I was part of the move to have it named in his honour.

Michael Duffy became Attorney-General in April 1990 just at the time the position of CEO of the Family Court was being permanently filled. The appointment was to be made by the Governor-General on the recommendation of the Chief Justice according to the *Family Law Act 1975*. The Attorney-General's Department Secretary who had made me redundant opposed my appointment to the position and apparently gave certain advice to Michael Duffy which delayed the recommendation of the Chief Justice being put into effect. Michael Duffy later apologised to the Chief Justice for the delay saying that he had been wrongly advised both as to the facts and the law and the appointment then went through.

Duncan Kerr replaced Michael Duffy as Attorney-General in April 1993 but only for about four weeks and then Michael Lavarch was appointed. Michael was very good to deal with and had as his Principal Adviser Jon Stanhope who had previously been Secretary to the Joint Select Committee reviewing family law. Jon afterwards became Chief Minister of the Australian Capital Territory and later presented me with a medal and a certificate for 30 years community service as a Justice of the Peace. (It is now 41 years service).

Len in lighter moment with Attorney-General Michael Lavarch and Chief Justice Alastair Nicholson

In March 1996 with the Coalition back in power, Daryl Williams became Attorney-General. I had previously had a lot to do with him in his capacity as President of the Law Council of Australia. He had also invited me to present a paper on computers and the law at the 1987 Legal Convention in his home city of Perth. The paper was entitled 'Winds of Change in the Courthouse—Computers and the Courts' and was one of only five papers from the Convention reprinted by the Australian Law Journal'. If imitation is the sincerest form of flattery, I was highly flattered indeed by '*The Bulletin*' in its edition of October 13, 1987 plagiarising the paper without attribution of any kind.

The abstract of the paper reproduced in the Australian Law Journal reads:

> The paper sets out areas of potential application for computers in the courts and shows how the new technology has already found its way into courthouses. It discusses the likely future directions of computer technology in relation to courts in each area of activity and concludes that there is an inevitability about these winds of change despite the inherent conservatism of courts. Some aspects of the conflict between judicial independence, economic rationality and public accountability are discussed in relation to particular examples of technological opportunities.

Almost thirty years later I am quite happy with the accuracy of my predictions in that paper.

When Daryl Williams was appointed, the Chief Justice asked me what he would be like from the Court's point of view. On the basis of my previous dealings, I said that I thought that he was thoughtful, moderate and sensible and would be fine. What I didn't count on was his apparent antipathy to the Chief Justice which seemed personal and led to very rough times for the Court. Daryl seemed determined to weaken the power of the Chief Justice of the Family Court of Australia and carved the Federal Magistrates Court out of its jurisdiction. We had advised him strongly that it would be a mistake but he was determined. Experience proved it to be an expensive and ultimately failed enterprise. The two Courts eventually merged administratively but at greater cost than would have been the case if the Family Court had been left untouched.

Other Interesting Characters

I first met former Justice of the High Court, Michael Kirby, in 1974 when he was appointed President of the Law Reform Commission and I had a part in helping him set up the new body. We subsequently seemed to run into each other often in airline lounges around the world. When I was appointed CEO of the Family Court of Australia he sent me a kind note of congratulations. I had the opportunity to reciprocate when he was appointed to the High Court and ventured the opinion that it would prove to be a very good appointment. Always meticulous with his correspondence, he sent me a thank you note in response saying words to the effect that '*if anyone would know a good judicial appointment, you would*'. I have always admired Justice Kirby's great ability to master a wide range of subject matters, his erudite and entertaining speeches and articles and his outstanding flair for media.

Similarly, when Justice (later Sir) Gerard Brennan was appointed to establish the Administrative Appeals Tribunal I had a role in helping him obtain resources which he publicly acknowledged on an anniversary of the Tribunal. When he moved to the High Court and later became Chief Justice we maintained a very cordial relationship.

Among the many interesting characters I encountered over the years was Bert Taylor who was Chief Reporter of the Commonwealth Reporting Service. Bert and I had a good relationship but it was severely strained when he invited me to the Commercial Travellers' Association Club in Flinders Street, Melbourne, one night after work. After dinner Bert challenged me to a game of snooker. Half-way through the game I had a good lead and Bert said that he had to go to the toilet and that a club member who was watching the game would play a few shots for him until he came back. Time went by and this bystander was proving a dab hand at snooker. Bert didn't come back and I narrowly won the game on the black ball. He then returned and told me that the bloke playing for him was the Club champion. My reply was unprintable.

One downside of having responsibility for the Court Reporting Service was that the court reporters were covered industrially by the Australian Journalists' Association headquartered in Sydney. I discovered that negotiations there required me to consume half a dozen middies of beer during lunch. That was either the way that they did business or an attempt to put me under the weather beforehand; perhaps both.

After the *Family Law Act 1975* was enacted, Lionel Murphy set up an advisory committee to help establish the Family Court and it included Sydney barrister Ray Watson, later appointed a senior judge, and John Marshall, a district level judge from Adelaide who also became a senior judge in the Family Court. Rumour had it that Lionel Murphy had promised the Chief Judge appointment to both of them and possibly to several others as well but gave it to Elizabeth Evatt instead as the inaugural Chief Judge in 1976. I had quite a bit to do with advising the advisory committee. John Marshall had been hankering to visit the Northern Territory and asked me to arrange for him to go there on behalf of the advisory committee which I duly did. On the flight from back from Darwin to Alice Springs, a breakfast flight, I had the window seat and John the aisle. I vaguely noticed John talking to a rough looking character across the aisle. This bloke then reached into a battered

Gladstone bag at his feet and handed John a magazine. John handed it to me. It was pornographic. I asked John, *'What did you say to him.'* He replied, *'I said that my mate is a bit of perv; can he borrow one of your magazines?'* I called him some unprintable names. John was also noted for a joke he played on Justice Kemeri Murray when she joined the Court in Adelaide. She was a bit nervous on her first day of sitting so John gave her a number to call if she got into trouble. Sure enough, she adjourned the Court and dialled the number. It was 'Dial a Prayer.'

I first met Chief Justice Sir Garfield Barwick of the High Court of Australia while the High Court was domiciled in Darlinghurst, Sydney. The Justices of the High Court were housed in two floors of that building, the Chief Justice and more senior Justices on the upper level. I well recall Sir Garfield referring with some rancour to 'the downstairs cabal' led by Justice Lionel Murphy. At that stage appeals from the High Court of Australia lay to the Privy Council of the UK and Sir Garfield had been a Privy Councillor since 1964. I recall seeing a copy of a letter from him to Prime Minister Fraser saying simply, 'I am minded to sit on the Privy Council' in a particular matter. He did not regard himself as requiring approval and was simply informing the Prime Minister. Sir Garfield involved himself heavily in the design and construction of the new and permanent High Court building in Canberra and much of it reflects his opinions and tastes. He personally chose much of the artwork. A very strong albeit somewhat controversial character.

In 1979 with the proposed building of a new High Court in Canberra, Sir Garfield proposed that an official residence be built in Canberra for the Chief Justice of the High Court. That proposition was not supported by the Attorney-General but instead a 'Canberra Allowance' was accepted for Justices required to remove to Canberra because of the new building. I wrote the Cabinet Submission.

Al Grassby was a colourful character both in personality and dress and I had a good bit to do with him while he was Commissioner for Community Relations. (The cynics of the day described him as Paterson's Curse; colourful but absolutely useless to man or beast). There were always strong rumours of his Mafia connections and he eventually resigned after the report of the Nagle Commission. I once asked him not to give me any more favourable mentions in his annual reports to Parliament because it was not doing my reputation any good. He looked a little startled and unsure whether I was joking but he complied.

The Department was for a period plagued by sit-in demonstrations led by one Ray O'Shaughnessy during the Secretaryship of Sir Clarrie Harders. (There was no front door security screening in those days). On being warned that Ray was in the building, Clarrie would lock the door to his section of the Executive Suite and with great agitation telephone me to do something about getting Ray out of the building. On one occasion I diverted Ray to my office in the Executive Suite together with his rag-tag retinue. One lady had her small son there and the boy began to show alarming signs of needing to go to the toilet. I offered her the use of a toilet but she said, '*Too late! He just shat.*' Ray was charged from time to time with obstructing Commonwealth Officers in the performance of their duty and proffered the defence that, as they didn't actually do anything, there could be no offence. I was called to give evidence in one of his cases and appeared before Justice John Gallop in the A.C.T. Supreme Court. At the end of my evidence Justice Gallop thanked me for leaving a very busy job to give evidence in his Court. I wasn't sure whether he was joking as I had no choice under summons but to come.

While on the subject of serial pests, while I was running legal aid David Harold Eastman was a persistent applicant for legal aid in pursuing his fights against authority, particularly against the former Treasury Head John Stone who he said had forced him out of Treasury. His applications were generally unsuccessful and he took to telephoning the legal aid office, abusing the staff and swearing at them. I directed that his calls be diverted to me in future. Early in our first conversation he began to swear and I said, '*Mr Eastman, if you swear I will hang up.*' He did and I hung up. This pattern was repeated in a few more telephone calls until one day he swore and he hung up. Shades of Pavlov's dogs! I was greatly surprised when Eastman was charged with and convicted of the murder by shooting of police Assistant Commissioner Colin Winchester (whose wife Gwen worked in the Attorney-General's Department) as that seemed inconsistent with his previous behaviour. His conviction was quashed after nearly 20 years of imprisonment and the courts are currently considering whether he should be retried.

Jim Killen, who had entered Parliament in 1955 and who is credited with saving the Menzies government in 1961 winning his seat by 9 votes, once told me a story about his first Question Time in Parliament. Richard Casey (later Baron Lord Casey of Berwick) had approached him with a 'Question Without Notice' for him to ask in Parliament. Casey said that he wanted the question to be asked with a great deal of passion and emphasis. Killen eagerly complied. Casey rose to respond and said, *'That is the silliest question I have ever heard.'* Jim said that the next question he asked him really was without notice.

Soon after I joined the Family Court I was asked to go to Melbourne to speak to the Judges collectively about security matters. After I had been speaking for a while a senior judge, Harry Emery, who had been a commando captain during the Second World War, interjected in a derisive manner. I weighed up my chances, thinking that if I don't accept this challenge now I will be looked upon as a lightweight forever. I turned and savaged Harry. He just smiled. Years later over a drink in his hotel room while we were in Hobart, he said to me, *'You know, I made your reputation that day in Melbourne when you spoke to the Judges about security.'* He had done it quite deliberately to give me an opportunity to show what I was made of.

PART SEVEN
PARLIAMENTARY COMMITTEES AND ADVISING

Giving Evidence

An interesting part of my life from 1974 to 2000 was appearing before Parliamentary Committees. The most constant of these were Senate Estimates Committees but there were also Public Works Committees and Public Accounts Committees. There were other *ad hoc* committees such as the Joint Select Committee on Certain Family Law Issues that occupied huge amounts of my time from its inception in 1993.

The Joint Parliamentary Committee on Public Works provided some interesting experiences. This Committee sits to examine proposals for expenditure on major public buildings such as courthouses and office blocks. My earliest was at Alice Springs in respect of the proposed new Supreme Court Building there. It was one of my first building projects and the hearing occupied three days and two nights, most of which I spent giving evidence. Despite the supposedly objective nature of the inquiry, the opposition members were trying to show that the proposal was excessive and extravagant while the Government members aimed their questions at demonstrating the opposite. Over a beer at the Alice Springs Club on the first evening Bert James, the Opposition Labor Member for Hunter, asked me 'Is there any bloody question you can't answer Glare?' I replied, 'Yes there is Bert but you haven't asked it yet.' Bert was a former sergeant of police from the Newcastle area and was fairly well acquainted with courts. On the second day I spent a lot of time trying to justify the standard of fitout and finish that the proposal contained. That night again over a beer, Bert said to me 'Those bastards didn't know what you were talking about when you argued for the dignity and prestige of the courts. But I did. You can't hold a court in the chook shed among the chook shit now can you?' I said, 'Bert if you had told them that I wouldn't have had to answer another question!'

A significant feature of the Alice Springs proposal was that the old cell block was to be preserved alongside because of a campaign run by an elderly local lady, whose name if I recall correctly was Mrs Doreen Braitling, who argued that there were hardly any historic buildings in Alice. She was successful. The old cell block was extremely primitive and ring bolts were set into the concrete floor of the large open area that held the prisoners and they were shackled by leg irons to those bolts. When the new Alice Springs cells were built alongside the modern police station I inspected them with the Police Commissioner only to find that someone had faithfully reproduced ring bolts for leg irons in the cell floors. They were hastily cut off.

Bert James gave me another notable moment in Hobart when the Committee was examining the proposal for a Commonwealth Courts Building in Davey Street. He was nodding off quietly when the Chairman, Mel Bungey, noticing his somnolence, impishly called him to ask the next question. Bert awoke somewhat startled and looked at the magazine on his lap under the table. It happened to be a fishing magazine. Quick as a flash he asked 'Will there be any fishing cases heard in this building?' I replied, 'Mr James, I respect the authority of the publication from which you are quoting but, no.'

At that same hearing Michael Hodgman, a Tasmanian and a Federal Minister at the time, had offered to help me by giving evidence. Michael had the nickname 'The Mouth from the South' and I was concerned that he might talk us into trouble so I asked him not to help. He attended and gave moral support but I don't recall any evidence from him.

The hearing for the Family Court building in Goulburn Street Sydney had to deal with the arguments from the N.S.W. Bar Association that Goulburn Street was too far from the legal precinct and was therefore not appropriate as a site. This despite the fact that the Sydney Magistrates Court Building, the Downing Centre, was already adjacent. Philip Twigg QC (later a NSW Judge), who I knew quite well, represented the Bar. When giving evidence he said rather lugubriously, 'I have worked in these courts man and boy for 30 years' or words to that effect. Unable to resist, I interjected very quietly 'It shows Philip. It shows.' Although it was meant for Philip only, the microphones picked it up and everyone heard it. Laughter ensued and I was lucky to get away with it without a rebuke from the Chair.

The task of Senate Estimates Committees is to examine the budget figures of each portfolio before the budget is voted upon by the Senate. This can be a very detailed examination of particular aspects or a broader perusal, sometimes both in relation to different areas. These Committees each examine a group of portfolios and are chaired by a Government senator. My role from 1977 to 1990 was to represent the Attorney-General's portfolio as principal witness. From 1990 I was principal witness for the Family Court of Australia.

The task of principal witness is to lead the portfolio team and requires an extensive knowledge of the portfolio and its budget components as well as its senior personnel. Essentially, the aim of the Opposition Senators is to embarrass the Government through finding some questionable expenditure or policy flaw to expose the Government publicly. Senators usually have briefs prepared by their staff to guide them in seeking out these soft spots. If your Minister is not a Senator, another Minister who is a Senator represents before the Committee. Ministers representing usually say little unless the question is of an obvious political nature. The task of the principal witness is to provide the first response to questions, endeavouring to answer them broadly and in a way that does not open avenues for follow-up questions. I was instructed by my first Attorney-General's Department Secretary,

Clarrie Harders, to 'keep those bloody lawyers away from the microphone; they don't know when to stop talking.' If necessary, follow-up questions are referred to a specialist witness from the portfolio. The objective is to answer truthfully while not provoking further questions or providing ammunition to the questioners.

It was common to wait days for the call to attend a hearing, much of the time in Parliament House while other portfolios took their turn. Timetables for hearings were not fixed and often they went on into the early hours of the morning. My record was 5.30am. Examinations might be concluded within one day but often they flowed over to another day or days.

There was a good deal of humour to be had in Committee deliberations but it was necessary always to remember that it was not a good idea for humour to occur at a Committee member's expense. While it was acceptable to ask for a question to be repeated, it was certainly not acceptable to ask for it to be rephrased, a mistake I saw others make often and invariably it provoked a sharp response from the Senator concerned.

In later years when my hearing began to deteriorate it was sometimes difficult to be sure that I was answering the right question. This was made much more difficult on one occasion when Senator Nick Bolkus, who was a mumbler and had a beard that made lip-reading difficult, asked me questions while eating a banana. I thought perhaps he was speaking Swahili. I owe a lot to my faithful staff, particularly then Principal Registrar Ian Loughnan (now Justice Loughnan), who would quietly prompt me to make sure that I had heard the question properly. However, Ian tells the story that on one occasion he told me that I had answered the wrong question when Hansard later showed that I had for once got it right. There was sometimes advantage to be had by answering the wrong question. Senators often asked questions from a list prepared by their staff and, again, Ian tells it well. He said that I was asked a question which I answered with 'blue'. He says that the Senator looked at me then at the brief wondering whether that could possibly be the right answer before giving up and moving on to the next question.

To digress a little, Ian Loughnan while Principal Registrar came with me on his first visit to Darwin. I convinced him that, to experience the real Darwin, we should stay in the old Hotel Darwin rather than one of the new modern glass buildings. I explained that it even had a punkah, although no punkahwallah, as the cooling fans were operated by a motor rather than a man. (By way of explanation, in the colonial age, the word punkah came to be used in British India for a large swinging fan, fixed to the ceiling, and pulled by a coolie, called the punkawallah. To cover a larger area, a number of punkahs could be connected together by strings so that they would swing in unison as they did in the Hotel Darwin). Ian agreed but when we checked in I found that I had overdone the 'real Darwin' bit and we were assigned to the backpacker's section. Ian swears that a towel cost extra. It was rudimentary at best but we made the most of it. I had previously been coaching Ian in roulette during our travels so we went to the Darwin Casino, Ian dressed in smart jeans and reefer jacket. He was refused admission under the dress code because of the jeans. I doubt whether any other Judge has managed to be excluded from the Darwin Casino! On the day we were to leave Darwin our business was exhausted but we couldn't get a flight out until 12.30pm. Ian wanted to see Kakadu National Park and asked how far it was from Darwin. I replied that it was 230 kilometres. The Northern Territory had no speed limits on country roads in those days so we figured that we could leave early and be back in time to catch the plane. Borrowing a car from the local Registrar, we made it but I have to say there was not much time for sightseeing at Kakadu.

I once gave a talk about Parliamentary Committees to a Judges' Conference at the famous Mietta O'Donnell's Queenscliff Hotel on Port Phillip Heads in Victoria. An attendee was Senator Jim McKiernan who was at the time Chair of the Joint Select Committee on Family Law. After explaining the Committee process to the Judges I concluded by saying that I believed in it as a democratic exercise but my complaint was that Senators particularly were not well enough versed in the subject matter to be forensically efficient. Moreover, the reduction in details that followed streamlining of line items in the budget material gave them fewer clues as to areas upon which to focus.

After dinner at that Conference, we played some snooker and I was partnered with a Judge against Jim McKiernan and his staffer (for a $10 side bet). My partner was playing rather too well and I reminded him that Senator McKiernan held something like the power of life and death over the Court and perhaps this was a game we should not win. Later that evening, after a full complement of drinks, I was playing against a Queensland Judge and overbalanced slightly moving the white ball half an inch with my hand. I was going to replace it but my opponent insisted on the four point penalty. Justice Neil Buckley called to my opponent, 'You shouldn't have done that!' The game was down to the colours and, very incensed, I played as never before and cleared the table without my opponent getting another shot.

Diplomacy similar to not winning the snooker game once came into play when the Attorney-General's Department played the Chinese Embassy in a friendly basketball game as an adjunct to a visit by members of the Chinese judiciary. At an early time-out, I asked the Departmental Secretary, Pat Brazil, whether this was a game we should win. He said that, as it was the first such game, we could win it. We did and at dinner I was presented by the Chinese Ambassador with a piece of jade for man of the match.

On what was intended to be my last appearance before a Senate Estimates Committee, Hansard records the following exchange:

> **LEGAL AND CONSTITUTIONAL LEGISLATION COMMITTEE—09/02/2000—FAMILY COURT OF AUSTRALIA**
>
> **CHAIR** *(Senator Marise Payne)* —We move now to the Family Court of Australia, and I would invite officers from the Family Court to come forward.
>
> **Senator McKIERNAN** —I was looking forward to the appearance of Mr Len Glare at today's hearings and I find to my great disappointment that he has ducked out of it. That

was going to be his last day as the CEO for the Family Court of Australia before the Senate estimates committee. Why has he ducked out of it?

Mr Phelan —He is in Darwin assisting the Chief Justice with the opening of the new registry there.

Senator McKIERNAN —That is a very poor excuse for not appearing.

CHAIR —I am sure our Northern Territory colleagues, Senator McKiernan, would think it was a very good excuse.

Senator McKIERNAN —Could you pass on to him our very best wishes for all the services that over the years he has given to the court and to parliamentary committees such as this. I hope that our paths do cross at some time in the future. I think I would be speaking on behalf of everybody from the committee in saying that we do wish him well in his new role as a retired person or in whatever he engages in.

Mr Phelan —I will.

CHAIR —Thank you, Mr Phelan.

Advising in Parliament

One of the roles of a senior public servant is to advise Ministers on the floor of Parliament, both in the House of Representatives and the Senate. This might be your own Minister or the Minister representing the portfolio in the other House. The adviser sits in a box alongside the Ministerial benches and gives immediate advice to the Minister on request. This duty provided an excellent vantage point from which to learn how the Parliament actually functions.

Some of these occasions proved quite amusing. I have an abiding memory of Senator Reg Wright from Tasmania looking up to the Press Gallery and calling its members 'myrmidons and troglodytes'—that sent everyone searching for a dictionary. On another occasion my Director, Finance, attempted to join me hastily in the Advisers' box but he was very large and clumsy and fell into the box with a resounding crash.

Of course, anticipating possible Parliamentary Questions Without Notice (PPQ's) was a game played daily within every Department. Senior officers tried to anticipate what might be asked and prepare an answer which the Minister could give and thus appear very knowledgeable. This brief of PPQ's went every day to the Minister.

Some Ministers were occasionally a little the worse for wear after dinner and it was the adviser's unwritten task to contact the Attorney-General's staff to arrange an extraction if it looked like becoming a problem.

After the Coalition came to power in 1996, there were cutbacks in the Family Court's budget and I was asked by the Attorney-General to attend upon a group of Coalition backbenchers in Parliament House one evening to explain the cuts and their likely effects. This was because of strong constituent feedback to electorate offices. I duly attended and explained the cuts until one of them said, 'Of course, these are cuts made by Labor before the election?' I replied, 'No, they are cuts made by your Government.' A certain gloom descended on the proceedings at that point.

PART EIGHT
COURT SECURITY

Anticipating Trouble

I had a general responsibility for security within the Attorney-General's portfolio and by 1979 was becoming concerned in particular about the possibility of security incidents in the Family Court of Australia because of the highly emotional nature of the jurisdiction. I raised this concern in high level inter-departmental meetings but could get no support from anywhere about the need to increase security levels.

In June 1980 Justice David Opas, a judge of the Family Court at Parramatta, answered a knock at the front door of his home in Woollahra after getting up from the dinner table and was shot in the abdomen. He died from his wounds without regaining consciousness. This very much changed the security climate and all at once police were provided to guard every Family Court building in Sydney and to accompany each Judge to and from work in a Commonwealth car.

I was sent abroad to study security in courts and looked at the UK (including Belfast), Italy, Japan, U.S.A. and Canada. In London the IRA had been a problem for some time and I looked at the court security methods there. Their use of bomb curtains in government buildings was extensive. These curtains hung in loose folds into a box beneath the inside of the window so that bomb blast shattered windows would have the glass fragments held in the loose curtains rather than cause mayhem inside. Various methods of protection within courts were examined and I went to Lancaster to look at a high risk trial involving the man known as Mr Asia who was allegedly the head of a large drug syndicate. He was held in a gaol within Lancaster Castle and within the walls of the castle there was also an Assizes Court where the trial was to be held. There was intelligence to the effect that he had offered the IRA many millions to free him. This visit illustrated to me the fallibility of humans in the security area. On entering the castle the guard said he was sorry but everyone had to be searched. I was carrying a satchel which I held at arm's length while the security wand was waved over my body. I was then admitted without any examination of the satchel at all.

I had lengthy discussions with MI5 people about their work on building protection and bomb protection standards. Of particular interest was the need to use laminated glass to prevent fragmentation and the corollary was that the glass had to be fixed in very deep channels to prevent the whole piece being projected inwards.

MI5 arranged for me to go Belfast where I had discussions with the Lord Chief Justice of Northern Ireland, The Lord Lowry, who liked Australians. He explained to me in detail the threats facing his court and the methods adopted to defend against them. I was a little startled to see, outside his courthouse, a World War II type sandbagged post like a machine gun nest. The indoor security guards were carrying pump action shotguns. There had been many attempts on his life and a particular risk was for him and his Judges coming and going between Northern Ireland and the Republic of Ireland. Information on their travel was tightly controlled to minimise the risk of ambushes but nevertheless some occurred. He seemed quite sanguine about the personal threats, even after a bomb attached underneath his car fell off in his driveway while his daughter was driving. His main concern seemed to be that his bodyguard saw all of his bad golf shots.

My trip to Belfast involved a risk of another kind. I had been out to dinner with the ASIO representatives in London the night before and, despite having very little to drink, felt decidedly unwell the following morning. I took the Tube to Heathrow very uncomfortably where security was tight and eventually boarded a British Airways flight for Belfast. Breakfast was soon put in front of me and, to my horror, consisted of kippers that presented a very real risk given the state of my stomach. On arrival at Belfast I was picked up by an armed driver provided by MI5 who took me to Stormont Castle which was at that time closed to the public and housed the UK Northern Ireland Office. (I would not have felt so comfortable with the armed escort had I known at the time that the IRA regarded it as a point of honour to assassinate anyone under that kind of protection). After a briefing on Northern Ireland history and affairs, I was treated to lunch. Right in front of me was placed a huge and smelly Stilton cheese which again strongly tested my stomach.

While I was in Belfast a bomb exploded in the city centre, fortunately not near me. Barb, back in London, heard the news and had a worrying wait until I came back.

I returned to Belfast as a tourist in 2015 and looked at areas like Falls Road where parts of the high wall separating Catholics and Protestants have been preserved. Everywhere there are memorials and reminders of those troubled times but Belfast is now usually quite peaceful.

In Rome I had discussions with the police and also with an architect who designed the security measures for the court in which the Pope's attempted assassin, Mehmet Ali Agca, was to be tried. I learned something about Roman drivers when the armoured Alfa-Romeo police car in which I was being driven came to stop behind a private vehicle which had stopped at a red light. The police driver sounded the horn until the driver in front drove through the red light. Senior members of the Italian judiciary insisted that bombs were not a threat in Rome because it would be un-Italian to use them rather than something more personal like a gun or a knife. Soon after that theory proved to be wrong.

A pleasant diversion in Rome came when my architect contact threw a party at a restaurant behind the old Roman baths for a newly appointed Chief of Police. My ASIO escort scared me considerably on the way there by driving the wrong way around a narrow one-way road with a high stone wall so that visibility was very limited. Surviving that, the party started about 9pm and Möet champagne flowed endlessly in the outdoor garden setting. About 3am the party broke up and I was taken to see the famous Trevi fountain. However, at the time of the morning no water was flowing and there were drunks and drug addicts draped over it.

Of interest in the USA was the design of courts and the emphasis placed on traffic path segregation, that is, keeping separate circulation paths within the courts for judiciary, prisoners, public and staff. I was helped by the US Marshal's Office in relation to a number of areas including personal protection for judges under specific threat. They took me to Baltimore, Maryland, to a particular courthouse without telling me anything much about the nature of the excursion. While sitting in the body of a courtroom, my escort suddenly asked me 'Are you carrying?' Not catching on quickly, I asked 'Carrying what?' He said 'Are you armed?' I assured him that I was not and it then emerged that I was about to witness a courtroom hostage demonstration with people acting parts. He had been suddenly concerned that I might shoot an actor. The demonstration proceeded quite realistically and included hostage negotiation.

In Columbia, South Carolina, my escort was a genuine Southern Colonel (an ex military one as distinct from the honorary ones). He was very informative and a real delight to work with. When I bought him lunch he said in a lovely southern accent, 'You shame me boy!' It was shortly after the visit to Columbia by former Prime Minister Malcolm Fraser who had been presented with a Civil War rifle as a memento. According to the media, he had previously had another notable experience in nearby Memphis Tennessee as well, something to do with losing his trousers. The locals tactfully avoided too much mention of that. Upon viewing the Capitol building in Columbia,

I noticed six gold stars affixed to the exterior. Instead of repairing the marks made by General Sherman's Union Army cannonballs during the civil war, they have been marked by gold stars as badges of honour.

On return home I drafted minimum security standards for court buildings including traffic path segregation, entry screening, window treatment, undercroft protection, placing of ducting and air intakes in non-public areas and the avoidance of simple slab construction that could collapse like a pack of cards if a bomb was strategically placed as happened with the Brighton Hotel where the UK Conservative Party conference chaired by Margaret Thatcher was being held in 1984. They also covered surge control at entrances in case of demonstrations. I wrote protocols for the personal protection of Judges, their homes and families as well as their travel to and from work. The measures included silent telephone numbers, no publication of addresses and monitored security systems.

Worst Fears

In March 1984 much of what might have seemed academic became quite real when the home of Justice Gee of the Family Court at Parramatta was bombed and he was injured. One month later a bomb exploded outside the Parramatta Family Court at night. It caused damage but no injuries. Then four months later a tragedy occurred at the Greenwich apartment of Justice Ray Watson. As he was leaving for work one morning, his wife Pearl accompanied him to the door, opened it for him and a bomb placed against the door exploded killing her instantly. Justice Watson was also injured but not seriously. The saddest part for me was that a few weeks earlier he had asked me to come to his house to advise him on security. I had noted that his front door was inside an unlockable foyer which screened anyone or any object in the foyer from being seen by other tenants. I said that he should keep it locked but he said that the Body Corporate would not allow it. I suggested that he ignore the Body Corporate and do it anyway. It had not been done by the time the bomb was placed in that precise location.

I had the task of informing Attorney-General Gareth Evans who was at that time in China at Xian, the site of the entombed warriors. I spent an hour endeavouring to make a telephone connection with him until, at last, Beijing connected me to Xian. Just then the telephonist's shift changed in Beijing. All connections were broken and I spent another hour re-establishing contact. Gareth subsequently sent me a cable via Foreign Affairs to meet him in his Parliament House office at 5pm on 9 July 1984 and to bring Chief Judge Elizabeth Evatt. I picked Elizabeth up from the residence of Professor Leslie Zines in Canberra and we met Gareth.

These events raised the security temperature in the Family Court very considerably.

I knew that the NSW police suspected an Italian born industrial chemist and were pursuing that lead seemingly to the exclusion of other possible suspects. While the chemist was excitable and voluble and regularly made threats, it seemed unlikely that his personality profile matched the offences. It also seemed to me that all the offences were the work of one person as were several non-court incidents relating to parties and relatives in certain Court proceedings. I wrote to the Australian Federal Police Commissioner on 12 February 1985 linking these events and several others to one person. I wrote, 'I understand that (name deleted) was one of the suspects under consideration by the Bomb Task Force but that their attention is centred more directly on other suspects.'

The AFP reply of 10 April 1985, two months later, said that 'a definite motive for the bomb incident of 10 February (the placing of a car bomb in a vehicle outside the former residence of the solicitor for (name deleted) former wife cannot be determined'. In relation to my request that (name deleted) be kept under surveillance, '...surveillance (is) a manpower intensive operation ... must be considered with other priorities....'

My request for surveillance was triggered by concern for the safety of two Sydney Australian Legal Aid Offices that had granted legal aid to the particular person's former wife in view of the car bomb attack that appeared to be aimed at the legal aid solicitor. Logically, if the perpetrator was pursuing all those who assisted his wife, those offices could be at risk.

In July 1985 the Jehovah's Witness Hall at Casula was extensively damaged by a bomb during a service. One person was killed and many injured.

Some 30 years later, while writing this book, a report appeared in the Canberra Times of 30 July 2015 carried the headline 'Suspect charged over family court bombing.' The body of the report revealed that a man had been charged with the offences relating to the Court and also with other non-Court incidents, some of which I had detailed in my letter. Apparently he had been charged with 32 offences including four murders and one attempted murder. I have copies of my correspondence with the Australian Federal Police.

Security screening was introduced at the main entrances to all Family Court buildings and photographic identity cards issued, programmed to allow the judiciary and staff to enter specific areas. My wife called to see me one day in my office in the Sydney court building. She was much amused while going through screening to see a woman have to surrender a small jar of vanishing cream to the guard. She wanted to know whether he thought the woman might disappear.

I had some trouble with the union insisting that buildings be evacuated for every bomb threat. At that time telephone threats were practically a daily occurrence. I wanted to introduce a limited self-search by staff to see whether any objects that did not belong were inside rather than evacuate as a first response. My logic was that, if I wished to harm staff, I would first make a couple of hoax calls to establish where the evacuees were to assemble for the customary roll call and what paths they would use to get there. Then I would simply place the explosive device at the assembly point or along the traffic path. With that method I would never have to enter the building and risk being identified or recorded on CCTV. I was never able to convince them and, fortunately, neither scenario came to pass. The union officials' reasoning seemed to be that they would never be criticised for evacuating even it was not the best course.

I had for some years been advocating increasing Family Court formality by the use of wigs and gowns and raising the Judge's bench above floor level as is the case in other courts. I reasoned that formality depersonalised the

Judge to some extent and would reduce the risk of reprisal. Gradually these changes were accepted.

As a frequent spokesman and public figure for the Court, I was exposed to threats and risk myself and had to take similar protective security measures to those taken by the Judges.

PART NINE
OBSERVATIONS ON PUBLIC SERVICE

Lessons from Experience

Reviews of the public service have been endemic for as long as I remember. Of course, they much pre-dated my employment. As part of my studies in Public Administration I looked at the UK Northcote-Trevelyan report of 1854. Many others followed and continue to this day. It reminds me of what is said about the weather. Everyone talks about it but no one does anything. In my view, very little improvement has come from these reviews.

I recall in the early 1950's that Prime Minister Menzies announced his intention to slash the public service, by 10,000 jobs if I remember correctly. Such broad intentions have been announced many times since. Arbitrary cuts have many unintended effects and few lasting benefits. Governments tend to prefer broad measures, such as the so-called efficiency dividends, because they avoid the Government having to make selective decisions about which services to cut and leave the hard work of such decisions to the public service. If heads of Departments suggest specific cuts to Government it is often regarded as a political trap because they would have to take the responsibility. Instead, broad-brush approaches such as the efficiency dividend Governments find more appealing.

I have dealt with the subject of performance pay earlier in this book. Outsourcing was another vexed policy issue. During the 1980's Government began to embrace the idea of outsourcing some services to the private sector on the basis that they would be done more cheaply and efficiently. Information technology was a prime target. Many of us in the public sector cautioned against this on a number of grounds. We said that unless we retained in-house capacity we could not easily reverse the process if it proved to be not as efficient as was hoped. We said that once the specialised capacity was transferred to the private sector we could be held to ransom through price increases every time a contract was renewed. We also said that we would have much less internal capacity to monitor services provided to us. It was likely that IT staff working for Departments would be hired by contractors winning tenders to supply IT services to the same Departments but at far greater salaries. All of this happened.

Similarly, buildings owned by the Government and occupied by Departments and other government bodies were sold off and leased back to Government. This was equivalent to selling the farm. It can only be done once. While providing a temporary budget boost, the general experience was that after a few years the overall cost was much greater, comparatively, than before. This demonstrates one of the problems of annual budgeting and three year terms for Governments. Longer term effectiveness is overlooked for short term apparent or political gains.

I have previously mentioned the abolition of central control of establishments resulting in classification creep and inequities of pay for the same work across Departments.

Recently there has been strong talk of a move towards a bureau approach to shared services and the probability of locating some of those services offshore. Sharing of services such as finance and human resources is superficially attractive but it removes from senior managers the advantage of having a close relationship with people able to advise on such things. That, I think, will lead to managers having less regard for the implications of their decisions in those areas as well as to the making of decisions without proper consideration of those specialised effects. It will also mean that people with those background skills will not reach management levels in the mainstream. In any case, I have a philosophical objection to offshore outsourcing because it reduces employment within Australia.

Being a public servant of the old school (by definition), I believed strongly in giving impartial advice whatever I thought of the politics of a proposed policy at the time. Someone once said to give a Minister advice that you know he doesn't want to hear on a certain matter once is obligatory. Twice is brave. Three times is suicidal. These days it seems that many public servants shape their advice to suit the politics of the party in power and never give advice that might be unpopular, even the first time. 'Can do' advisers seem to be sought by the less discerning Ministers who think that they are then better served than they would be by impartial expert experienced advice.

One of the things that I learned from working with Ministers over the years is that, no matter how good your relationship, when it comes to the crunch you will readily be jettisoned to preserve the Minister's position. If it is to be the Minister or you, it will be you. The best protection against this is to document anything involving a Minister so that there is a record of what occurred and the Minister cannot deny involvement. You may choose to call it a paper trail or backside protection; it is the only effective protection a public servant has from being blamed for a political disaster.

PART TEN
FAMILY COURT OF AUSTRALIA

Shaping a New Administration

As mentioned previously, I took up duty as the first Chief Executive Officer of the Family Court of Australia on 1 January 1990. On this date the Court became self-administering and was no longer a part of the Attorney-General's Department. However, the Court had previously required very few staff with administrative skills and the first task was to set up a structure and recruit the people to fill it. The Court had previously been headed by a Principal Registrar appointed for legal rather than managerial skills. This was a very intensive activity for some months. I had the advantage of living away from home because the head office was located in Sydney and I was able to put in the very long hours required.

On my first day there arrived on my desk several boxes full of applications for a position of Court Officer in Brisbane, a very low level position. These applications had not been processed at all and were simply sent to me for decision. When I enquired why such a matter had come to my desk I was told that all such matters had come to the Principal Registrar previously. I sent them back to Brisbane for local decision. Similarly, I found that decisions of all kinds were referred to the CEO without summary, comment or recommendation. I sent most of them back for lower level decision or at least a recommendation as to a course of action. It took a little while for staff to get the idea that they could not simply refer everything to the top. If they could do that, then there would be no point in having them at all. It did not take long for them to adapt to the new way of working.

I was operating out of Sydney and the Chief Justice out of Melbourne. Not ideal, but we soon got it working. I had previously served on the Council of the Australian Institute of Judicial Administration with Chief Justice Alastair Nicholson and we had several other interactions over time. The division of labour between us was that he controlled all judicial activities and I reported directly to him about the administration of the Court. However, I held all the financial and human resources powers under relevant legislation and was not subject to direction by the Chief Justice in the exercise of those statutory powers. Under the Family Law Act, he did have the power to give me a general direction but our agreement was that, if he found it necessary to do that, he would have my resignation. We had a great working relationship for the more than ten years that I was there.

Alastair was, and still is, a very egalitarian character with a strong social conscience and a lifelong interest in ordinary people. It was my task to advise him as to possible negative effects on the Court, particularly politically, of his public pronouncements. He usually sent me his draft speeches to vet before he delivered them and almost always accepted my suggestions for changes. However, if he really wanted to say something contentious that he knew I would advise against, he simply did not give me the speech until after he had delivered it.

Once when we were in Perth, Alastair and I were invited to the home of the Deputy Chief Justice, Alan Barblett, for dinner. Alan was a former Olympic hockey player for Australia, a very good bloke and an excellent host. We drank some good wines and had a great night. On returning to our Sheraton Hotel in the city, we found ourselves opposite an Irish pub and called in for several pints of Guinness by way of a nightcap. We had arranged to go jogging about 6.30 the following morning. I was just getting ready when the telephone rang. It was Alastair, obviously feeling the pinch a little, suggesting that we call it off. In a fit of bravado, I told him to please himself but that I was going anyway. He said 'you bastard' and came too. After a kilometre or so along the bank of the Swan River it became obvious that he was struggling a bit. I told him that I would go on ahead and sprinted a few hundred metres to the next bridge and then rested behind it. After about ten minutes I sprinted back past him again, much to his amazement. When he retired I was invited to write an article about him for the Court's magazine and I confessed in it to the trick I had played on him. He was much amused and had never suspected it.

In 1993 I attended the Commonwealth Law Conference in Nicosia, Cyprus, and Barb came with me. We were placed in a hotel at Limassol on the south coast and commuted across Cyprus each day to Nicosia for the Conference. Cyprus was divided and the north was occupied by Turkish Cypriots; the south by Greek Cypriots. Across the middle of Nicosia was a buffer zone patrolled for a long time by Australian police. At the end of the conference we took a week's leave and embarked on a cruise from Limassol, to Haifa in Israel, Port Said in Egypt and back to Limassol. The vessel was the *Princess Marisa* and it was anything but a luxury liner. At each stop we went ashore and in Israel went by bus from Haifa to Tel Aviv to Jerusalem. In Jerusalem we saw the historical places so familiar to us from the Bible including Bethlehem and the Wailing Wall or Western Wall of the second temple. While visiting the Knesset (Parliament Building) it was sobering to see school excursions arriving with parents rostered on duty with Kalashnikovs to protect the pupils.

In Egypt we went by bus down to Cairo and saw the pyramids and Sphinx at Giza on camel-back. Barb's camel driver wanted me to give him more money or he would make her camel gallop, thus scaring her. I refused saying wives were easy to get. It took a while to be forgiven for that. Our bus was protected by truckloads of soldiers in front and behind but one such bus was nail-bombed a few days later. We also visited the fabulous treasures of the Cairo Museum.

Len at the Great Pyramid in Egypt.

While the Joint Select Committee on Certain Family Law Issues was operating, we had much pressure and a huge workload. Roger Price MP became Chairman of the Committee in 1995 and had a very jaundiced view of the Court. We spent enormous amounts of time preparing submissions, responding to questions and giving evidence to the Committee. For weeks at a time I slept in the office, finishing work about midnight and starting again at 5am. In June 1995 Roger Price was replaced as Chairman. After several years of this pressure, the process ended with Kevin Andrews MP saying that the Court should be left to concentrate on its functions rather than being distracted by constant inquiries. Roger Price finally told me that he had tried his hardest to bring me down personally but now conceded defeat.

One of the interesting features of the Court was the mixture of disciplines that it encompassed. There were 55 Judges, 7 Judicial Registrars, 80 lawyers, 140 Counsellors (psychologists and social workers) and several hundred administrative staff. These were scattered around the country except for Western Australia which had its own court under the *Family Law Act*. The patterns of thought and work among these groups were disparate indeed. I used to joke that I could do all of their jobs with a one line question:-

- Judges—'and what authority do you have for that proposition?'
- Registrars—'and what order do you seek?'
- Counsellors—'and how did that make you feel?'
- Administrators—'has it been done before because nothing can be done for the first time?' (Apologies to Sir Humphrey Appleby).

Considering the mixture of these different disciplines, the Court came to work quite harmoniously with each group respecting the others' contribution to the common cause.

The key to success in such a bulk jurisdiction is keeping away from Judges those cases that really should not require a judicial decision. That was largely the work of the Registrars and Counsellors and they were very good at it with the experience being that only about 5% of cases required judicial determination. This made the Judges' workload manageable, at least to a reasonable degree, and kept cost and disruption to the parties down. Case management was being continually refined during my ten years with the Court and I know that it has developed further since.

The Nature of Family Law Jurisdiction

I learned a great deal about human nature while with the Court, although some of it I would rather not have learned. Divorce is a very bad time in the life of most people who undergo it and intense emotions are evoked in many cases. Few divorces are totally amicable. Often the parties are at different stages in their desire to separate; in many cases one party does not realise or perhaps admit that there is anything wrong in the marriage when the other party wants it terminated. The two main areas of contention are the children and money. Often there is a desire on the part of one party to punish the other for actual or perceived behaviour. This can lead to prolonged disputation far beyond what is reasonable. Some fought over their joint assets to the point that they spent all of their net worth on legal fees. The fact that the Family Law Act does not consider fault as a ground for divorce removes the possibility of a party being able to consider themselves vindicated by a judicial ruling. Unfortunately, often the children are used to punish the other party by making contact difficult. It is a most complicated and emotionally charged jurisdiction.

As CEO I made it a practice to see all complaints and to reply personally to a great many of them. This led me to look at the detail of many cases which gave me a good understanding of the nature of marital disharmony and its aftermath. Many of the stories were tragic. In some extreme cases the children were murdered by one parent to punish the other. However, I have to say that listening to one side of a story is not a good way of gauging truth and that it is virtually impossible to know what happens between two parties in a marriage. A trend had developed of asserting sexual abuse against fathers in many cases as a tactic to oppose contact and 'punish' the ex-partner. Similarly, I suspect that some apprehended violence orders were sought for tactical reasons although no doubt many were valid.

Occasionally there was some humour. One elderly lady wrote about an article on proceedings in the Court that she had read in the *New Idea*. She had been shocked and wrote, 'they wouldn't be allowed to print it if it wasn't true would they?' I had to disillusion her by saying that the story was not factual. Another complainant railed against the power of the Court to grant divorce saying, 'What God has joined together let no man put us under'. I believe the correct quotation is 'let no man put asunder' but his version has a certain appeal.

Against the advice of the Court's Marshal on security grounds, I once met with ten men from a men's organisation whose members had been through, or were going through, family law proceedings. One by one they told appalling stories of how their spouses had treated them and how unfair it all was. In the end I observed aloud that they must be the worst judges of human nature in Australia as every one of them had married the worst woman in the world. Nevertheless, I often felt some sympathy for the situation in which some people found themselves through no apparent fault of their own. Of course, as I have already observed, who knows what actually happened in the marriage?

International Experience

The Court gave me a great deal more international experience. I attended several conferences of the international Association of Family and Conciliation Courts and delivered papers at most of them. Perhaps my finest paper was entitled *'Benchmarking: An Emerging Strategy for Family Courts?'* delivered in Montreal in May 1995. It received great critical acclaim internationally. When visiting Capetown, South Africa, some months later, a woman Magistrate who had been at the Montreal Conference showed me a paper distributed by her Chief Magistrate on the same subject. I was surprised to find that it was my paper with a few *mutatis mutandis* alterations. She watched me closely for a reaction and I simply observed, 'He writes well doesn't he?'

After South Africa I visited Zimbabwe where I had been asked by their then Chief Justice, Tony Gubbay, to give advice on court administration. That turned out to be fairly unprofitable because their systems needed computerisation but with high levels of unemployment and very low wages they could do things more cheaply manually and create employment at the same time.

Barb and I took a week's holiday while there to visit several game parks. We visited Victoria Falls staying at the famous Victoria Falls Hotel and had a helicopter flight over the falls. We did an elephant back safari from there concluding with feeding the elephants and having champagne in the open air viewing a beautiful sunset. Barb complained that my elephant, which hers was following, continually broke wind. That was the least of her worries because, as we went through the shallows of a lake, her driver told her to hang on because there were crocodiles in the water. I think that he would still have her fingernail imprints in his ribs.

At a smorgasbord in a Victoria Falls hotel one evening I asked the server what kind of venison a dish contained. He gave me a big smile and said, 'Wart hog sir'. It tasted OK.

From Hwange National Park, where we stayed in Sable Lodge and Sikumi Treetop Lodge, we had been scheduled to fly to Lake Kariba but President Robert Mugabe commandeered the airliner and we had to go back in a decrepit van to Victoria Falls to catch another flight. Apparently this was a common occurrence and we were told that he once took over an international flight on their national carrier in Europe, emptying out all the paying passengers to make room for himself and his entourage. On Lake Kariba we took a canoe safari through hippotamus waters and a walking safari through lion country. One morning there was a hippo in the courtyard of our apartment.

We also visited the ancient ruins of the Great Zimbabwe.

Zimbabwe was a wonderful country from the point of view of game parks but sad in the social and political sense. Inflation of the currency was rampant.

I was to fly back to Johannesburg from Harare and from there to Vancouver to deliver a paper on 'Courts and Indigenous Communities' at the conference of the Association of Family and Conciliation Courts. We flew into Johannesburg on Saturday afternoon and went to the South African Airlines lounge to await transfer to the United Airlines plane to Vancouver via San Francisco. After some time an official of South African Airlines approached and stated that he had taken our baggage off the aircraft. When I enquired why he said that we required a visa to enter the USA. I was flying on a diplomatic passport and in any case Australian citizens did not ordinarily need a visa. He was unconvinced and I suggested that he telephone the US Embassy. He said that it was closed on Saturday and that we would have to wait until Monday which would have been too late for the Vancouver conference paper. No amount of argument worked so I asked him whether he could fly us instead to Heathrow in London on our tickets. He said yes but that we would have to purchase tickets from London to Vancouver so I did that. Before leaving I wanted to find out his identity but his ID card was reversed. I reached over and turned it round saying that he had been so helpful that I would like to write and thank South African Airlines. Having got his name, we then went to Heathrow arriving at about 6am on a Sunday.

On presenting at the United Airlines counter, they looked at the tickets and said in effect, 'What the hell are you doing here? You don't need a visa for the USA.' We were agreed on that and so we were able to go on directly to Vancouver where we arrived sooner than we would have via San Francisco. It was Barb's birthday and I told her that not every girl gets taken to London for her birthday. She was not impressed as we didn't leave the airport.

South African Airlines eventually gave me an apology and a refund but I wondered what would have happened to a traveller who didn't have access to enough credit to solve the problem. I have not flown on South African Airlines since.

I once attended an international conference at Baden Baden in the Vienna Woods near Vienna in Austria. The English language sessions were over-subscribed and there was a call for volunteers to change to the French language sessions. I rashly volunteered and then spent three days working very hard to understand the proceedings. I found the use of abbreviations especially trying but was helped by a French-Canadian lady who filled in the gaps for me. During the conference Barb took the light-rail into Vienna but could not understand the German language instructions on the ticket machine so she sat with money clutched in her hand hoping to find a conductor. Instead she was accosted by several ticket inspectors who gave her a hard time and fined her the equivalent of AUD$300. We subsequently took a tour of Schonnbrun Palace where she told the woman guide of her plight. The guide kindly arranged a refund for her.

One interesting local East Austrian custom was that small *Heuriger* taverns with special licences had their own vineyards and when their new wine came in they placed fir or conifer twigs in a circular *Buschen* over the door. When supplies ran out after two or three weeks they closed. In that period they also served food. *Heurig* means 'this year's.'

On one occasion my domestic airline ticket was drawn at random and I won a 10 day tour of USA national parks and canyons. It was not apparent whether the winning ticket was on private or work business so I used it to get us to the Conference of Family and Conciliation Courts in San Diego and subsequently took the holiday tour. It started in Las Vegas and covered such things as the Navajo Nation territory in Arizona, the Grand Canyon, Bryce and Zion National Parks in Utah, Jackson Hole Wyoming, the Yellowstone National Park, the Dakotas including Mount Rushmore, Cheyenne the capital of Wyoming, white water rafting on the Shoshone River and ended in Denver Colorado.

Tour of National Parks and Canyons.

The Grand Tetons, Wyoming.

International Experience 199

Spirit of Wyoming statue, Cheyenne

Mt Rushmore, South Dakota

Opryland Hotel, Nashville Tennessee

Barb and Len in Bahamas

Public Service Equity Awards 1997

Indigenous Initiatives of the Court

The Family Court under Chief Justice Nicholson took a number of initiatives to bring its services to Aboriginal and Torres Strait Islander communities. One of these was to appoint Indigenous people within the Court to liaise with those communities. It was a very successful program and as a result I had the honour in February 1997 of receiving, together with Sydney Registry Manager Jennie Cooke, on behalf of the Court, the top award in the fourth annual Public Service Equity Awards from Dr David Kemp, Minister Assisting the Prime Minister for the Public Service.

Another initiative of the Chief Justice was to engage with the seven Cape York peninsular indigenous communities. We flew from Cairns to Bamaga in a small plane taking with us supplies for a community barbecue. We also met with community leaders in each of the settlements to discuss the Court's services and listen to feedback. One of the local indigenous leaders told me an amusing story arising from his employment as an extra in the movie 'Crocodile Dundee'. He said that when he arrived on location for each shoot they painted him black because he was not considered dark enough for the film.

The article in the Canberra Times *acknowledging 50 years' service.*

Fifty Years Service

On 22 December 1999 I completed 50 years of public service. Being tipped off by my children, the Canberra Times ran a lengthy article on this milestone. The heading was, '*Brilliant* public servant notches up 50 years service'. This got me some doubtful comments from colleagues and friends but resulted from the Chief Justice, Alastair Nicholson, being quoted in the article as saying that he regarded me as, 'a brilliant public servant whose attitudes typify all that is best about the public service tradition.' The article went on to say that my children had organised a huge hamper to be delivered to me with a message 'Fifty years in the public service! Love from your greatest admirers. Good on you Dad.'

East Timor

Just after the Indonesians left East Timor in a devastated condition, Chief Justice Nicholson was asked by Jose Ramos Horta if he could help with restoration of the courts and justice system in East Timor. Bill Jackson, the Court's media advisor who had been an aid worker in Portuguese-speaking Mozambique, and I went to East Timor as an advance party for the Chief Justice and Justice Neil Buckley to complete the delegation. We flew from Darwin to Dili in a US Air Force C130 transport plane. On arrival at Comoro airport in Dili, we were greeted by an RAAF Squadron Leader who called out jokingly 'Welcome to Comoro international airport'. Nothing at the airport was functioning, no airlines, no staff, no customs or immigration control. Our first task was to find out how to get to Dili. No transport was operating and the Indonesians had destroyed virtually all vehicles before they left. One of the Australian rental car firms had brought a few 4WD vehicles over and we were fortunate to find one of them just returned to Comoro so we took it over. We drove into Dili and saw total devastation. All buildings, however humble, had been torched. Almost every roof had collapsed. The next task was to find somewhere to set up camp before we made contact with the CNRT (the Portuguese acronym for the Council of National Timorese Resistance) which was the nearest thing to a government that East Timor had at the time.

We stumbled upon the ruined Hotel Turismo and the owner, on hearing why we were there, said that we could have one room and would not take money. The room had no power, no beds, no windows, no furniture but at least the floor above kept the rain out. We had taken in some food and water to keep us going until we could locate supplies. The Australian Army provided us with drinking water.

Bill and I set out to make contact with the CNRT which was the peak local body for the several resistance movements and met some of their key people. Their legal person, Ana Pessoa Pinto, became our liaison officer and guide (she was also the former wife of Jose Ramos Horta and had been a judge while in exile in Mozambique). A brave lady, she was suffering malaria at the time but stuck with us throughout.

We then set out to see for ourselves what state the city of Dili was in and also made a video record which was later professionally edited.

Dili had previously had a population of about 200,000 people. Many were killed and others fled the city. Some went to West Timor. Over a period of about a month after the ballot for independence from Indonesia every building—shops, houses, schools, offices—had been looted and the stolen goods taken back to Indonesia. Powerboards, copper wire, vehicles, furniture, household items and anything else that could be carried away was taken. Nothing was too small! Then each building was sprayed systematically with fuel and set on fire. This happened not just in Dili but over the whole country. Livestock not taken were shot.

The slogan was painted on buildings, 'You can have your country back but eat rocks'.

All the banks were destroyed so people had no access to their money or even to financial records. Land titles from 1975 on were destroyed so ownership of land could not be proved. Schools had no books or writing materials or desks and chairs. Virtually no one was employed.

Many people had been killed and we saw rough graves beside houses. Some 400 people were burned alive in one building. Another massacre occurred among people seeking sanctuary in the Santa Cruz cemetery. We met a priest who had 100 orphans in his care and he was just one of many. Bodies were left lying all over the country and there was not even a program to pick them up.

I have an abiding memory of the beautiful curious children who came out to greet us wherever we went.

When the Chief Justice and Justice Buckley flew in a couple of days later we met with UN officials under the leadership of Sergio Veiero de Mello who was later killed by a bomb in Iraq. Our delegation inspected what facilities were left and gave such advice as we were able. We also subsequently arranged for essential supplies for the courts to be sent in by container.

We flew back to Darwin in a RAAF Hercules.

I was later approached by then Justice Marcus Einfeld of the Federal Court of Australia on behalf of Australian Legal Resources International to return to East Timor after my impending retirement to advise on the restoration of the justice system. After I had received my vaccinations and bought a survival kit, Justice Einfeld suggested that, as I would be receiving superannuation, I would not need remuneration for this task. I thought that risking my life and health deserved some recompense so we parted ways.

Media

Dealing with the media over the years created some interest and many hazards. I underwent media training in the mid 1980's and learned some of the tricks of the trade but experience taught a lot more. Radio interviews were vastly preferable because they were almost invariably live and offered little opportunity for chicanery by the media. With television, most of it is pre-recorded and this allows for all kinds of manipulation. The most unscrupulous is asking you a question, getting your answer and then varying the question before cobbling your previous answer to it for the broadcast. I found many TV interviewers/presenters quite unscrupulous. Over sometimes hours of tape they would try to drag from you a 'grab' that they could use adversely. The sneering tone of the voice over presenter then came into play to try to present you in the poorest possible light. As far as I can see, many television journalists are without ethics or scruples and I regard them as a very low form of life.

Newspaper journalists were rather better but not many could be totally trusted to do what they agreed to do. One I found very trustworthy was the legendary Paul Kelly of *The Australian*.

Television interviews using a single camera offered some diversion. The interviewer would ask you all of the questions with a camera trained from behind them on the subject. The camera would then be reversed to focus on the interviewer who would then do what they call 'noddies' pretending to acknowledge your answers. The noddies would then be spliced into the tape. I occasionally got some juvenile amusement by trying to make the female interviewers laugh during noddies.

Statutory Senility and Retirement

When I reached the age of 65 I encountered what I call statutory senility. At that time the position of CEO of the Family Court of Australia could not, under the *Family Law Act 1975*, be held by a person aged over 65. The Chief Justice could, however, appoint me to act for a period not exceeding 12 months which he duly did. Then it was a matter of deciding whether I should stay the whole term or choose an earlier date of retirement. I chose to retire at the end of April 2000.

On my last day at work the Chief Justice circulated an email to judicial officers and staff. It read in part:

> Today is the last day that Len Glare occupies the position of Chief Executive Officer of this Court. Len joined us in 1990 and pioneered the introduction of the system of independently administered Courts. He came to us from the Attorney-General's Department, where he had been Deputy Secretary. ... I can say that the work undertaken by him in this Court involved almost constant absences from his home, extraordinary and punishing work hours and an absolute dedication to this Court and what it seeks to achieve. He has never hesitated to give advice even if it might be thought to be unpopular with me or other Judges

and I have greatly appreciated this. It is an approach which in my view accords with the finest tradition of the Public Service. In accordance with the same tradition, if I have not accepted his advice, he has always backed me to the hilt. His service to the Court has been exemplary and we will all miss him.'

With Chief Justice Nicholson

Pat Brazil, former Secretary of the Attorney-General's Department wrote of me in similar vein in 1989, 'There is a determined side to his character, which has meant on occasions taking a stand on particular points that to some seemed inflexible. His judgment often proved to be right in the longer term ...'.

My retirement function was held at the Hyatt Hotel in Canberra on 20 May 2000 and had a large attendance from people and representatives of organisations that I had worked with over the years as well as my extended family and friends.

One of the guests was His Excellency Dr Bhadra Ranchod, then South Africa's High Commissioner to Australia, with whom I had become friendly at the gymnasium. Bhadra also had some professional dealings with senior Judges of the Family Court. My long time friend Harry Kwong, who was then working post-retirement from CSIRO as a Court Officer in the Family Court, was the Master of Ceremonies and I thought we might have an international incident on our hands when he told a joke about an Indian lady whose husband scratched the red dot on her forehead and won a car. Bhadra is of Indian heritage. He did not take it amiss but was called back to the High Commission during the evening because Fiji had suffered a coup by Fiji nationalists, essentially against the Indian population having political power.

I received many messages and letters on retirement. Most of them were kind although one from the Auditor-General, Pat Barrett, left me wondering. He remarked how much he had 'appreciated your friendship and your unique way of doing business.' Unique?

A nice letter came from the Hon. Justice Michael Kirby of the High Court of Australia. It read in part, 'Our association goes back to the first day of my appointment as an officer of the Commonwealth in December 1974. At that stage, you were in charge of many of the activities related to establishing the Law Reform Commission. I will never forget the help that I received from ... you ... . Your work since then in the Australian Institute of Judicial Administration and for the United Nations, as well as lately in the Attorney-General's Department and most recently in the Family Court displays the very best qualities of the officers of the Commonwealth, as Robert Garran conceived them at the foundation.' I greatly appreciated his comments.

From Judge Pat Mahony, Principal Family Court Judge of New Zealand, 'When one thinks of the tremendous achievements made by the Family Court during your term as Chief Executive with Alastair as Chief Justice, they can only reflect on the great partnership which together you formed. The bold innovations which you made and the uncharted areas which you explored have had an impact on the whole of the Court system in Australia and beyond.'

From Justice Linda Dessau, now Governor of Victoria, 'Len, I wanted to say 'farewell' and a personal thanks for all your careful work on our behalves. I have enjoyed watching your competent approach to delicate and difficult issues and appreciated your help and advice on many occasions.'

PART ELEVEN
FAMILY

Siblings

Family has always been important to me. In the early part of this book I described the lives of my parents and my siblings growing up in a remote area with an impoverished but happy family. The values our parents gave us and the sense of self-worth they imparted to us seems to me to have led us all to make something of our lives. Each of my siblings had no expectation of entitlement and earned their success through their own efforts.

My story has been told (assuming you have read this far.) My younger brother Kel has perhaps a more remarkable life story. He had several years as a clerk in the office of the Shire of Karkarooc at Hopetoun after leaving school and then in 1957 joined the Victoria Police. After some years as a fingerprint expert he decided to commence a law degree part-time at the University of Melbourne. (He was possibly inspired by my mature age tertiary study on the basis that if I could do it, anyone could!) However, the Police hierarchy at the time did not favour tertiary qualified policemen and he was 'banished' to run the Russell Street Police Complex dining room. He qualified LL.B. (Hons) despite attempts at discouraging his academic journey. A change of heart seems to have then occurred in the hierarchy and his law qualifications were put to use as a specialised prosecutor and then in charge of prosecutions at Preston and Prahran Courts. From there his career blossomed and he progressed quickly through the senior ranks becoming Chief Commissioner in 1987, retiring from that post in late 1992. In his police career he received seven commendations for outstanding performance. He was awarded an AO in the Order of Australia in 1993, the Order of St John in 1990, and the Australian Police Medal (APM) in 1986. Post retirement he became Executive Chairman of FBIS International Issues Management Pty Ltd and a Director of the Heidelberg Golf Club. He also practised as a barrister and solicitor. As I was more practised in management, Kel sometimes used me as a sounding board on management issues and we had many discussions while he was Chief Commissioner. He published his autobiography aptly entitled *The Angry Ant* in 2015 (Dewey Number 363.2092).

My youngest brother, Rob, trained as a primary school teacher at Ballarat and then taught in far-flung country schools for a number of years. His teaching career culminated as Principal of the Ferntree Gully Primary School, a large Melbourne suburban school. Having long been interested in Union affairs, he gradually became more and more of a full-time Victorian Teachers' Union operative. He spent some years as the General Secretary in Victoria of the Australian Education Union and is a life member of that body. He is happily retired at Mulwala NSW, a short distance from the Yarrawonga Golf Club where he spends quite a bit of time. Unfortunately, both my brothers are better golfers than me.

My sister, Janine, fourteen years younger than me, married Graeme Poulton, the son of a local Hopetoun farmer. Graeme eventually joined the Victoria Police and served in Melbourne and as Inspector at Swan Hill. They then acquired the historic White Swan Hotel at Swan Hill and Janine came into her own running a large and busy hotel for some years. She was an extremely capable manager. When they sold the hotel Janine became a local real estate agent. Graeme then got a job as Regional Manager of the SES in Melbourne so they moved there for a time and then he transferred to become Regional Manager in Bendigo until retirement. Janine had been working for Brimbank City Council in Melbourne and commuted daily from Bendigo for a few years until her retirement. These days they are what Janine refers to as 'grey and orange nomads', the orange being a reference to her hair colour.

Ross in his Morgan Cheetah

Children

My own children have given me great cause for pride. The eldest, Ross, left school prematurely against my gratuitous and mistaken advice and became a computer operator with Defence. Largely by teaching himself, he progressed rapidly in information technology in both the public and private sectors. (I suspected when he was about eight years old that he had some gifts in that area when I came home from work to find the television sound had been rewired to come out of our radiogram). After being a very well remunerated IT consultant to Customs for some years, he has joined Lockheed Martin. Ross has his own light aircraft and once managed to crash on landing at Goulburn airport with me on board when the weather unexpectedly turned very bad.

Second son, Travis, did not know what he wanted to be after finishing college so he enrolled in Science at the Australian National University. He finished his undergraduate degree and then thought that he should get some experience in research techniques by volunteering at CSIRO. He showed such promise that they put him on a Graduate Diploma by Research. When he finished that, he began a Ph.D. in Microbiology from ANU but also spent some time at Cornell University in the USA. Having met a New Zealand girl also doing her Ph.D. at Cornell, he then moved to Christchurch and worked as a research scientist for the Ministry of Agriculture and Fisheries and then AgResearch. He became a Professor at Lincoln University and was then promoted to Director of the Bio-Protection Research Centre at Lincoln, the South Island's only national Centre for Research Excellence. A renowned international figure in his field, he frequently speaks around the world, has written a number of books and holds nine patents.

Four Generations; Len, Travis, Nyssa and Nikolia.

Third son, Scott, had declared early on that he would never follow in his father's footsteps and join the Public Service. He worked as a casual in several Departments including the Attorney-General's Department when I was Deputy Secretary. While he was working in the Supreme Court Library, I went to pay a formal visit to the Library and the staff went to great pains to prepare a morning tea complete with silver service. He was astonished and told them 'It's only Dad'. Scott worked in a food distribution business for a while and did a back-packing tour of the world. Fate intervened and he did in fact join the Public Service, progressed extremely well, and is now a highly regarded Senior Executive. He was recently sponsored by his Department for a Master's Degree in Administration which he has completed.

Family at Scott and Megan's Wedding.

Only daughter, Kylie, went to St Vincent's Hospital in Sydney to become an Enrolled Nurse. I well remember taking her up to Sydney to settle her in and giving her a few hundred dollars to keep her going until payday. A few days later she asked her mother could she have more money because she had spent it all on making the room feel like home. Ever practical, Barb said, 'Why didn't you just throw some clothes on the floor?' When she graduated Kylie expressed a desire to work in Euthanasia. We suggested to her that perhaps she was thinking of Ethiopia. Kylie became a specialist in theatre at Canberra Hospital until she left to work as a medical claims assessor for NRMA to get more convenient hours for raising her daughters. Unfortunately, her car was rear-ended while she was on the way to work and she was unable to continue working because of her injuries. After seven years in the courts pursuing her claims, she eventually won in the High Court but had to endure great stress for all that time.

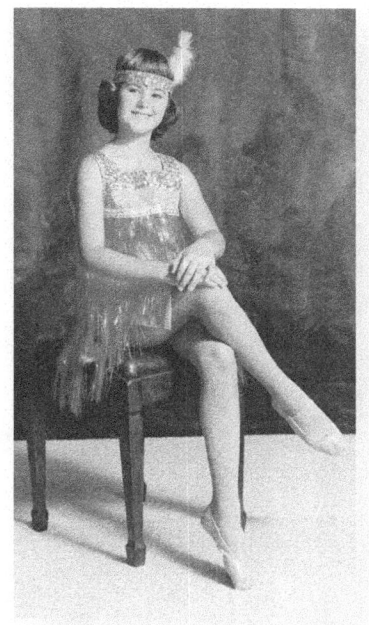
Kylie in ballet days

PART TWELVE
POST RETIREMENT

Keeping Busy

Some of my problem about what to do in retirement was solved when Barb joined me up as a member of the local Belconnen Magpies Golf Club. During my working life I had not taken up golf because I didn't think it fair to spend the weekend that way when I was not at home during most weeks. Barb seemed to think that she had married me for better or worse but not for lunch.

Len's Golf Trophies from RAAF Reunion Tournaments

Rotary Golf Charity Tournament, Len with Des Walsh and Lynton Dixon.

I also became President of the Rainbow Cottage Early Childhood Centre for a few years and re-wrote their Constitution.

An early retirement task was to add another floor to the house and that kept me busy although I engaged a builder for most of it. My daughter was living in an investment house that I owned but her family's needs were expanding so I took out an owner-builder's licence and extended that house considerably. I had previously added a wine cellar to my house underneath a new sunroom and I had found that the bobcat could not reach very far over the foundations. With the help of a hired pneumatic drill, I excavated the remainder by hand and carried out the soil and rock in buckets. That wine cellar has been a source of joy and comfort ever since.

My eldest son Ross vacated another of my investment houses and I spent three months refurbishing it and preparing it for sale. The time spent proved worthwhile when it sold for a good price and easily.

In 2001 I was awarded a medal for the Centenary of Federation, probably because I had spent more than half of the hundred years since Federation in the public service. At a ceremony in the Great Hall of Parliament House, I was presented with the medal inscribed,

IN RECOGNITION OF CONTRIBUTIONS TO THE AUSTRALIAN PUBLIC SERVICE ON ITS CENTENARY—19 JUNE 2001.

In 2002 I was awarded an OAM in the Order of Australia, presented by Governor-General Peter Hollingworth. I also became a life member of the Order of Australia Association. My talented daughter-in-law, Christine Wilde, mounted my new medal together with my military service medals, both the full size medals and miniatures. She also mounted my numerous Masonic decorations. All of this was free of charge but she has forbidden me to accept any more medals.

Presentation of OAM 2002 by Governor-General Peter Hollingworth.

In 2007 Barb and I took a tour of Canada and Alaska, a combination of cruising and land touring. It was a marvellous experience and Barb especially enjoyed it. Highlights included salmon fishing off Vancouver Island in Canada where we caught a very large king salmon. The boatman dressed it for us and one side fed eight people at a restaurant that night. The Butchart Gardens on Vancouver Island were amazing as was the Columbia Icefield on the mainland. Alaska was wild and beautiful but how the people who remain there during the winter survive (its population swells dramatically in summer) I cannot imagine.

Butchart Gardens, Vancouver Island.

Lake Louise, Alberta, Canada.

Tour of Canada and Alaska 2007

Glacier Bay, Alaska

At Captain's Table on Sapphire Princess

My Great Loss

I was afterwards very glad that we had taken the Alaska trip because Barb became ill after our return and spent months attending specialists who tried to diagnose the cause of her extreme pain. That was never adequately established but the treatment involved massive doses of strong pain killers over a long period and she became progressively more ill. On 4 May 2008 she became quite ill and very confused and our daughter Kylie and I took her to Canberra Hospital emergency. She refused to let us pack a bag for her because she did not intend to stay in hospital. She was admitted in the early hours of the following morning and was judged to be extremely ill. She was at first put in a four-bed ward. Then because of her grave condition she was placed in a private room. After one day there the staff told her that they had a very ill patient who needed the room and, being the woman she was, Barb readily consented to return to the four-bed ward saying 'of course; her need is greater than mine'. She was soon moved back again after a 'code red' breakdown in her condition. The doctors then told me that she was suffering multiple organ failure and would not recover and that kidney and liver transplants would not be feasible. Over the next week we prepared for her death and family and friends came to pay their last respects. I slept in a corner of her room each night. Tough and uncomplaining as always, she hung on and died on 14 May 2008.

The funeral was attended by more than 400 people and overflowed the chapel. Our four children and our eldest grandchild, Cara, gave courageous eulogies. Not knowing what else to do, I carried on with life as best I could and tried to do for the family some of the things that Barb had always done, like family dinners and Christmas day lunch and dinner. She had been, in Kylie's words, the glue that held our family together but we have managed to continue to be a close family in spite of our great loss.

Grandchildren 2012

Granddaughter Cara's Wedding

A by-product of all this was that, having helped Barb with her catering business and culinary masterpieces over the years, I had acquired a good deal of cooking knowledge without realising it and practice since has improved my competence. Barb had worked in a cooking school with many great Australian and international chefs and I inherited a magnificent cooking library, many of the books autographed.

Soldiering On

I had joined the Rotary Club of Belconnen in 2002 at Barb's urging and quickly became quite involved, first as *Bulletin* Editor and then as a Director. Club Directors run areas of Rotary Programs and I mainly handled Community Service. In 2007 I was approached about becoming President but I told them that I was too old and too deaf for the task. When I told Barb this she told me that I had to do it so I agreed to be nominated. She had gone by the time I became President in 2009 and the Club rallied strongly round me. I unexpectedly became President again in 2012/13 when a President resigned after one month in office and I have been pressed into service again for the year 2016/17. I have twice been made a Paul Harris Fellow by Rotary International. In Rotary I have enjoyed the company of like-minded people who really do give back to the community unstintingly.

In 2012 I visited China and stayed in the Australian Embassy in Beijing with fellow Rotary Club member Haida Passos and her family. Haida organised a very fine experience for me and I was busy sightseeing the usual tourist things like Tiananmen, Forbidden City, Great Wall and Ming Tombs. Among other things, Haida sent me to a Hutong cooking school and on a bicycling tour of Beijing. When the cycling people found out how old I was they gave me a solo tour with two guides and a camera crew, I suppose to promote that old people can do this too! We danced Scottish reels and drank Scotch one evening at the British School with a Chinese man playing bagpipes. I even got my first ever maniped (nails and toenails). Being keen to avoid Chinese toilets wherever I could, I failed to eat and drink enough one morning and passed out in the subway train carriage. An ambulance arrived and I quickly found myself on a stretcher with an IV tube in my arm. What worried me was that the ambulance was an old VW Kombi van, I wasn't secured to the stretcher and the stretcher wasn't secured to the ambulance floor. I had visions of old comic movies where the stretcher flies out the rear doors and goes careering down the street. However, no damage occurred and a battery of tests at the International Medical Centre (utilising my comprehensive travel insurance to the fullest) established that I was quite healthy.

At Rotary Club of Beijing.

Forbidden City Beijing.

At Great Wall of China, Mutiamo.

Cuban themed party at the Australian Embassy Beijing, Haida on the left and Kim, her American friend.

British School, Beijing.

Cycling Tour of Beijing.

As Rotary President.

While President I arranged for my Rotary Club to support the project 'Garden of Delights' at Cranleigh School for handicapped children where Barb had worked for 22 years. The Club contributed $35,000 to help convert a derelict area to a wonderful undercover playground specially designed for children with handicaps. The School displays there a memorial plaque to Barb.

An interesting voluntary task as a Rotarian was to go to the Kintore Aboriginal Community in the Northern Territory near the Western Australia border, about eight hours in a four-wheel drive vehicle west from Alice Springs. Together with another Rotary Club, my Club was involved in providing a dialysis centre at Kintore, called the Purple House. Partly because of genetics and partly because of diet and alcohol, there is a high rate of kidney disease in that area. Previously the residents had to travel to Alice Springs for treatment which was needed several times a week. The distance was too great to return in between treatments and many of the people languished and died so far from home. Provision of dialysis treatment within the Kintore Community has greatly improved the situation. We also established a bush medicine garden and a vegetable garden with an automatic watering system within the grounds of the centre. One of my tasks was to assemble 42 flat packs of furniture for the Centre. Unfortunately, before we arrived the nurse's husband had opened seven packs and couldn't assemble them so my first seven packs were a gigantic jigsaw puzzle with all the pieces mixed up.

We had been promised sleeping accommodation in the official accommodation blocks but there is apparently a pecking order and we, as mere volunteers, were 'gazumped' by visiting Centrelink staff. Luckily the nurse and her husband kindly gave three of us beds in their own home.

When I was searching for a spare part for something in the centre, I was told to go to Bunnings. I wondered why on earth a large commercial operation like Bunnings would be at Kintore. It emerged that Bunnings is the local term for the garbage tip where you really can find almost anything.

The Purple House.

Kintore view.

The township itself was littered with rubbish, particularly food packaging, plastic bags and bottles. When I enquired why no one disposed of their rubbish properly I was told that it was 'white man's rubbish' therefore not their problem, even though they were the consumers of what created the rubbish.

While at Kintore I visited one of the 'outstations' located out of the central community. Apparently a policy was developed to take people out of the main communities back to their grass roots locations by creating outstations. These were equipped with housing, power generation equipment, radiotelephone and cars. All of those outstations in the Kintore area have failed and people have chosen to live in the main community. The facilities have been abandoned and vandalised or cannibalised for parts and equipment. The cost must have been staggering. It reminded me of other communities I had seen where good houses had been built but abandoned after someone died in them. Better awareness of cultural factors would make for better planning and less waste.

I looked in the Kintore store to see what sort of food people bought there. To my astonishment the freezer was full of packaged kangaroo tails. Apparently it is not so easy to find kangaroos near Kintore.

I became a Senior Consultant with a Management Consultancy organisation but have not actually taken on much of that work. That came about when I met Nola Ann Hennessy at an Australian Institute of Management focus group and discovered that she was the founder and Principal of Serenidad Consulting. On gradually learning of her background, I nominated her for a Rotary Inspirational Women Award and she became a New South Wales State finalist. She had already written two books and subsequently her autobiography, *The Peace Angel*, won the North American Booksellers Award in the inspirational books category. It has since won numerous other awards including two for best autobiography. Nola's company now has a base in Texas as well as Australia.

As a consequence of joining Serenidad, I needed to take out a basic security clearance from the Commonwealth, my high level clearances having lapsed on retirement. This was an on-line process and required responses to many questions. One was to list all the countries I had visited together with dates. When I got to 40 or so countries I thought that enough was enough. I had been to the USA 20 times! I was also required to list all the people I had contact with in each country. I have a good memory but not that good. Then I had to give the dates of birth of my parents. When I entered those dates the screen flashed 'Warning! This is more than 100 years ago'. I didn't need a computer to tell me that! A very frustrating exercise.

In retirement I have maintained my fitness routine. Golf twice a week, tennis once a week and spending an hour and half in the gymnasium on each of the other days. I have had a lifelong passion for active sports and that has always been part of my work/life balance. It seems to pay off and my health remains excellent. In my early 60's I learned that keeping fit can be very useful. We were camping with friends in Bournda National Park on the New South Wales south coast. By coincidence, my son Ross and his family were camping in the same park. Barb and I were walking on the unpatrolled beach one morning while Ross's second wife and his daughter, Cara, were swimming in the ocean when a rip caught them. They rapidly got carried out to sea. Ross went after Cara who was the furthest out. I asked for help from all the young fit-looking fellows on the beach who suddenly became non-swimmers. Having not swum seriously for some years, I had no choice but to strip to my underwear, remove my hearing aids, and go out for Ross's wife but was quite sure that I could not make it back again. I reached her quickly with the aid of the rip and, fortunately, she did not panic but took hold of my shoulder as told. Utterly exhausted, I made it back to the last breaker on the beach and stood up only to be knocked flat by a final wave. Our friends on the shore dragged both of us to safety. It took me a day to recover.

I met Linda Baldwin in 2012 when she joined Rotary; in fact she was inducted into Rotary by Kalyan Bannerjee the world president, an unusual occurrence.

Linda on induction into Rotary by World President Kalyan Bannerjee with Mrs Bannerjee and Club President Lynton Dixon

Linda had lived in many parts of Australia and had spent a year touring the outback. We found that we had a lot in common, became friends and married in August 2014. We did not announce our intention to marry but went to Caloundra on the Queensland Sunshine Coast for the annual gathering of my siblings. On arrival at the house we had jointly rented I handed to my siblings and their spouses invitations to the wedding which was to be two days later. To say that they were surprised would be an understatement. After the ceremony I emailed my children to tell them. Travis responded, '*What is the world coming to! My father elopes*'. It took some time for Kylie to forgive me for not telling her beforehand; daughters are different! My family had suddenly grown to four children, two step-children, eight grandchildren, ten step-grandchildren and two great-grandchildren.

When we returned to Canberra and announced the event at our Rotary meeting there was a good deal of astonishment. I suspect some were thinking

Soldiering On 245

Len and Linda RAAF Reunion at Wangaratta

Len and Linda Wedding 2014

that I was far too old for Linda. I am very fortunate to have her companionship in the final part of my journey through life.

For my 80th birthday in 2014 my children gave me a great party with many guests, family, friends and colleagues past and present. The highlight was a video entitled 'The First Eighty Years' put together by my eldest son Ross with his commentary over covering my life thus far, the implication being that there were eighty more years to come. Hence the sub-title of this book.

Linda and I toured the United Kingdom and Ireland in May/June 2015, the first time in that part of the world for Linda. We began with eight days in London, then south to Dorset/Somerset/Cornwall (in the hope of warmer weather), north through Wales to Caernarfon then by ferry to Dublin. From Dublin south to Avoca then north again to Belfast in Northern Island via Newgrange in County Meath. From Belfast we toured the Giant's Causeway and the Coast Road on the way back to Belfast. From Belfast by ferry to Cairnryan in Scotland then across to Newcastle-upon-Tyne on the east coast of the UK all in one day. A couple of days operating from Morpeth in Northumberland with a Canberra friend, Peter Oldham, as guide then back to London for the

Filming Doc Martin, *Port Isaac, Cornwall.*

Soldiering On   247

Linda with 'Bert' from the cast of Doc Martin

Port Isaac, Cornwall

Chelsea Flower Show. Three more days in London (excursion to Windsor Castle, Bath and Stonehenge) then north again through the Cotswolds, York, Edinburgh, Pitlochry to Oban. South to Gretna Green, Nottingham, Stratford-upon-Avon then back to London via Suffolk (where some of Linda's ancestors originated) for the journey home. Linda's main lasting impression of the trip was that we travelled too far too quickly. *Mea culpa*!

Highlights included theatres in London (*The Mousetrap*, Shakespeare's *As You Like It* at the Globe Theatre and the final night of *Miss Saigon*), the outdoor Minack Theatre in Cornwall, Hampton Court Palace, Jorvik Village and the Minster in York, thatched cottages in the Cotswolds, changing of the guard at Buckingham Palace on the 70th anniversary of VE Day and much beautiful scenery, particularly in Scotland. We visited the Ferguson Clan House, Dunfallandy, near Pitlochry as part of my ancestral pilgrimage. In Port Isaac, Cornwall, we stumbled into the filming of an episode of the TV series *Doc Martin*. Port Isaac is very beautiful and Linda had her photograph taken with one of the cast. In Northumberland we visited Hadrian's Wall and several castles. On the final day back in London we made a memorable visit to the Victoria and Albert Museum.

We stayed mostly in Bed and Breakfast establishments arranged through Airbnb. At our first in Dalston, an inner north-eastern suburb of London, our landlord suggested that we go to a nearby Turkish restaurant for dinner. He mentioned that two famous London artists, Gilbert and George, dined there virtually every night and that they were always dressed formally in suits. The place was crowded and by coincidence Gilbert and George sat at our table. They have recently toured Australia and were featured in several newspapers.

PART THIRTEEN
A FORTUNATE LIFE

Reflection

With such a long and varied life and career, I have wondered whether I should make some observations that might help others just starting out. Perhaps that is the ultimate vanity. Alternatively, it might serve to help others avoid the pitfalls I have encountered; that might perhaps be a nobler objective. In any case, I have recorded what it was like to live in a remote location in those early days and those memories of the times would otherwise be lost to my family and to posterity. I have also recorded early telecommunications experiences.

My philosophy of a working life is very simple. Learn something from every job you do however much you dislike it at the time. Take the boundaries of every job as wide as you can. Be fair; people will allow you to be wrong occasionally so long as your approach is honest and you are fair.

Do not seek to advance yourself by denigrating others. Self-serving remarks are easily seen for what they are. Give your subordinates credit for their good work and take responsibility yourself for their mistakes.

I have lived by the rule that I do what I think is right whether or not it is popular. I have found that many unpopular views I have expressed became popular in the longer run.

In dealing with people, I have tried to find common ground across which to build a communication bridge, something personal and common to both of us. Perhaps mutual friends, a sporting interest, a shared history or experience – anything to establish a connection. I believe that most people are well intentioned and, with encouragement and opportunity, will give their best. Berating people in front of others is very counter-productive and is generally counter-productive anyway even when done privately. Insisting on formality does not help. First name use is not demeaning and if you need to be called 'Mister' to establish your authority you have already lost the battle.

Inevitably there will be people failures despite your best endeavours. In the public sector over the years it has been extremely difficult to fire under-performers. When the formal inefficiency proceedings route was taken, the person instituting the proceedings became the defendant and as a result most avoided the process. (I actually succeeded on the two occasions I used it but it was difficult, slow and required a great deal of persistence and the ability to deal with accusations and innuendo about your motives. The process had to be meticulous or it was thrown out on the technicality rather than the substance). Subterfuges were used more widely. One was to give untrue references to try to 'sell' the candidate to another unsuspecting agency. Most common was to abolish the job held by the person to make them redundant. Managers need the courage to play it straight and tell the truth but the balance of the system needs to be improved. I don't know how much this has changed since I retired, if at all.

One thing that I observed in the latter part of my career was that there is a certain kind of woman who likes to collect 'senior' scalps. I noticed that Judges were frequent targets for seduction and that even I as a lowly CEO was not immune. I can't convince myself, try as I might, that it was because of my good looks and charm. The problem, apart from morality, is that once a man succumbs to such temptation he is forever in the power of the woman concerned. I did observe a number of occasions where just that happened to senior men. An excellent early warning mechanism I enjoyed was the protection of several senior female colleagues, among them Angela Filippello and Carole Brown, who realised what was going on much earlier than I did and actively discouraged the females concerned.

Sometimes an odd human reaction occurs when you go out of your way to help people. They resent the fact that they had to be helped and blame you for making them feel that way. For example, a youngish lawyer in the Attorney-General's Department was caught allegedly taking drugs. He had a young family and needed to get away from the Canberra drug scene. I negotiated his transfer interstate to a new job instead of starting disciplinary proceedings. In later years, when I became CEO of the organisation I had transferred him to, it became very evident that he hated me and went out of his way to try to cause trouble for me. Such is life!

On reflecting on my life's journey I am reminded of Albert Facey's excellent autobiography, *A Fortunate Life*. Albert's origin was in Mallee country like mine albeit his in Western Australia rather than Victoria. On my retirement I received a letter from Justice Ann Robinson who reminded me that we had shared a car when she was first appointed as a Judge of the Family Court of Australia. Quietly using her legal forensic skills, she had extracted from me some information about my early life in the Mallee. In her letter she observed that I had a lot in common with Albert Facey. Similarly, my Rotary colleague and friend Lynton Dixon, a native of Western Australia, after hearing my short biographical talk to Rotary, thereafter insisted that I was Albert Facey reincarnated.

I firmly believe that my life has also been fortunate. A wonderful upbringing, varied and interesting life experiences, extensive travel, a happy and loving family, good friends and good health. Things had to be earned because I did not have a privileged background but, importantly, the opportunities to earn them became available to me and I took advantage of them. I feel sad for those who never had opportunities.

I owe a great deal to my family, friends and many of my work colleagues over the years. Most of us are not very good at giving acknowledgments at the time so this is my belated attempt to remedy that deficiency.

My life journey may in some respects seem improbable but it is certainly not unique. Many other people have come from similar origins and experienced great changes in their lives. Perhaps my story will create echoes for some others in their own lives. For my family and future generations there will be a record of vanished times probably beyond their imagination. Given the gene pool from which I spring, I may well be around for a long time yet but I wanted to write the story thus far in case I cannot later on.

We will see what another eighty years brings.